We Bow Down

Written by
Five Christian Ladies

Publishing Designs, Inc.
Huntsville, Alabama

Publishing Designs, Inc.
P. O. Box 3241
Huntsville, Alabama 35810

Second Printing, February 2004
Third Printing, October 2013

Printed in the United States of America

ISBN 0-929540-28-X

Contents

Foreword 5

In Memory — Cindy Colley 7
    Passover 9
    Lord's Supper 19

On Bended Knee — Foye Watkins 31
    O Jehovah 33
    Through Christ 45

Thus Saith the Lord — Sheila Butt 57
    Prophesying 59
    Preaching 71

Tithes and Offerings — Gloria Ingram 81
    Percentage Giving 83
    Purpose Giving 97

Fruit of Our Lips— Jane McWhorter 109
    Joyful Noise 111
    Heart Song 127

FOREWORD

You worship that which you do not know
We worship that which we know
God is a spirit and those that worship him
Must worship him in spirit and truth.
—John 4:23-24—

Why encourage women to study about their worship and influence? Walk into almost any Christian assembly and observe that women outnumber men. When families enter the house of worship, mothers generally determine how the children behave—visiting the bathroom and water fountain, whispering, passing notes, distracting others, or listening and participating with other worshipers. Women set standards—whether in reverence or frivolity by their attitude during singing, praying, giving, preaching, and partaking of the Lord's supper. Women demonstrate their attitude toward Christ by their worship demeanor and their pursuit of things spiritual—and others are influenced.

But godly women do more. They view preparation for worship as a privilege. Sunday is a special time. One husband grew weary of the weekly battle in his daughter's room. She rebelled every Sunday morning because of the clothes her mother selected for her to wear. At last, the husband petitioned his wife: "Next week, will you and Chloe please arrange to have your Sunday morning fight on Saturday?" They did. Women who strive to please God in worship look for opportunities throughout the week to construct plans that will enhance their families' worship. Clothes are selected, shoes are polished, meals are planned. Through detailed preparation, every effort is made to eliminate stress. One modern woman complained of never having time to prepare her family, including two children, for Sunday worship. She was habitually late. She mentioned the problem to her grandmother who said, "I certainly do not understand. You have a washer, dryer, and every convenience. I washed clothes by hand, ironed without electricity, and prepared clothes and food for seven children and was never late for worship." Have priorities changed?

During worship godly women refrain from visiting friends in the nursery, using it only when necessary. On special days, they bring food early, so as not to disrupt Bible classes by traipsing up and down the halls and then coming into the assembly late. In a Christlike manner, godly women can train others to show respect for the one who died for us.

God has set eternity in our hearts and has so worked that we should be in awe before him. Solomon taught that hundreds of years ago in the third chapter of Ecclesiastes. Our spirits long to bow down in submission to the all-powerful creator. Women who refuse to acknowledge "eternity in their hearts" exist in a state of confusion, continually seeking to fulfill themselves spiritually without God.

Five Christian women have set their pens to instruct and encourage true and spiritual worship. The very tenor of *We Bow Down* reminds us of our utter dependence on God while living in a society that grovels before Hollywood and offers sacrifices in sports stadiums.

Godly women present powerful messages by bowing down before God. When women take worship seriously, the entire congregation becomes more reverential.

We commend to you *We Bow Down*.

Peggy Coulter
Huntsville, Alabama

In Memory

Cindy Colley

Cindy Colley delights in her many opportunities to serve the Lord by speaking to ladies' groups, and by teaching classes for ladies and children in the local church. She also shares her harvest of knowledge by writing poems and articles. A collection of her poetry is soon to be published as a gift calendar/planner. Her book, *Crown of Creation,* is in its third printing.

Cindy and her husband Glenn are home educators and members of *Memphis Home Educators* and the *Tennessee Home Educators Association*. They teach Bible and speech classes for home-schooled students and conduct seminars for the parents of these students. Their experiences with their children, Caleb and Hannah, influenced Cindy and Glen to write *Your Mama Don't Dance*. The Colley's have produced two cassettes of Bible verses set to music: *Hannah's Hundred I* and *Hannah's Hundred II.* A sequel is in production.

Cindy, daughter of Lee Holder and the late Johnnia Duncan Holder, is a native of Birmingham, Alabama. She holds a B.A. in communications from Freed-Hardeman College. She resigned from teaching English for the blessings of full-time parenting and assisting Glenn in his work as a minister of the gospel. They live in Collierville, Tennessee.

In Memory
Old Testament

Passover

The Salvation Story

The original Passover story is a historical drama the likes of which has never been seen (Exod. 11:4-6). After almost four hundred years of Israelite slavery in Egypt, Moses the great deliverer had been sent by Jehovah, as he spoke from a flaming bush, to the house of Pharaoh to demand the release of Israel. God had equipped Moses with miraculous abilities to establish his God-given authority. By the time Moses appeared before the throne of Pharaoh, however, the king was already frightened that the Israelites were becoming so numerous that they might create an insurrection. Pharaoh was not about to let the people leave Egypt, not even for a short pilgrimage into the wilderness for worship. At the hand of Moses, God sent nine devastating plagues on the Egyptians. While the families of Egypt were subjected to insufferable afflictions, the land of Goshen where Israel dwelt was protected from harm. The plagues were so destructive that Pharaoh pledged the release of the Israelites several times during the desolation. But each time God removed the pestilence, Pharaoh immediately hardened his heart and refused to allow the Hebrew people to go.

And so it was time for God to keep a promise. Jehovah had instructed Moses to go before Pharaoh with these words:

> Thus saith the Lord, Israel is my son, even my firstborn. And I say unto thee, Let my son go that he may serve me, and if thou refuse to let him go, behold I will slay thy son, even thy firstborn (Exod. 4:22-23).

And so God executed the final plague, promising Israel that as Egypt awoke to find all of its firstborn children slain, that not only would they be allowed to leave, but they would be thrust from the country (Exod. 11:1). God prepared his people for a hasty departure by instructing them to borrow jewels of the Egyptian, jewels which were freely given by those who respected Moses (Exod. 11:2-3). These jewels were taken as spoils in the exodus according to the great judgment of God upon the kingdom of wicked Pharaoh.

Against the children of Israel not even a dog would move his tongue.

God's second promise to Israel was that while every firstborn child in Egypt would be dead upon the morrow—and even the firstborn of the beasts would die—that against the children of Israel not even a dog would move his tongue (Exod. 11:7). God was drawing a promising portrait of stark contrast between those who were in a covenant relationship with him and those who were outside of the covenant. This was a portrait he would continually place before them as they wandered through the lands of the heathen and conquered the powerful Canaanite tribes on the other side of the Jordan.

Following the promise of safety, God issued some very specific and intelligible instructions to his people. Their safety on this night of vast Egyptian desolation was contingent on their following the commands of God. Exodus 12:3-13 details God's instructions to his people.

1. He specified a time for the instructions to be followed.
2. He instructed them to take a lamb for each household, or for two households if the households contained few people.
3. He detailed the criteria the lamb must meet.
4. He told them to separate the lamb from the flock until the fourteenth day of the month and then kill it in the evening.
5. He demanded that they paint the blood of the lamb on the side posts and above the door of their dwellings.
6. He gave regulations for the seasoning and cooking of the lamb, and even about the discarding of any leftovers.
7. He ordered the Israelites to be dressed and to have their shoes on with staff in hand as they ate in haste.

God wanted to see their faith demonstrated, carrying out the intricate details of his instructions. He wanted them to be ready, believing his word fully, anticipating the great exodus.

Verses 12-13 of Exodus 12 are the embodiment of the Passover:

> For I will pass through the land of Egypt this night, and will smite all the firstborn in the land of Egypt, both man and beast; and against all the gods of Egypt I will execute judgment: I am the Lord. And the blood shall be to you for a token upon the houses where ye are: and when I see the blood, I will pass over you, and the plague shall not be upon you to destroy you, when I smite the land of Egypt.

It was still dark when Pharaoh awakened to find his son, heir to the great throne of Egypt, dead. Imagine the shock and devastation that he felt as he learned first from his servants, then from the dwellings that surrounded the palace, and finally, from the darkest dungeons of his prisons that there was not a single house without a corpse. Imagine his regret as he looked into the lifeless face of his son and wished he had let them go yesterday, or better yet, when Moses first came before his throne. He didn't wait until morning to find Moses and Aaron; he sent immediately and ordered them to be gone, urging them to ask a blessing for him. Imagine his guilt as he entombed his son in the midst of nationwide mourning ceremonies, likely in a tomb constructed by the Israelites. The consequences of pride in the face of Jehovah are always much more grievous than the offenders could have imagined!

Pharaoh flung open the gates of freedom to the Israelites in the middle of the night.

Pharaoh flung open the gates of freedom to the Israelites in the middle of the night. I have been abruptly awakened on a few occasions to go on an emergency trip. My kneading trough was never among the essentials I hastily packed for such a journey! Yet observe that God had a plan for an expansive illustration using unleavened bread that would be for all generations. Notice verse 34 of Exodus 12: "And the people took their dough before it was leavened, their kneading troughs being bound up in their clothes upon their shoulders."

Picture a group of slaves—probably more than a million of them—gathering the jewels of the richest nation on earth and assembling their families, flocks, and herds to embark on the greatest freedom journey of history. Now picture one person in each household binding up a dough board containing a lump of flat dough in the folds of the robe she was wearing and walking several miles to safety so encumbered. When they finally stopped, the cakes were baked over the first fires of freedom for Israel in four hundred years. As they reflected in the wilderness on the amazing events of the past twenty-four hours, the massive slaughter in Egypt, the protection of the blood, and the road to the promised land, their source of sustenance was the flat cakes, reminding them of the haste of their deliverance. God had a plan for unleavened bread!

The Memorial

> It is a night to be much remembered unto the Lord for bringing them out of the land of Egypt: this is the night of the Lord to be observed of all the children of Israel in their generations (Exod. 12:42).

It is interesting to notice that God planned the yearly Passover feast, also known as the Feast of Unleavened Bread, prior to the actual occurrence of the original Passover. In Exodus 12:13-20, God detailed the activities that would occur yearly to remember the passing over of the Israelite houses as the great death plague was occurring in Egypt. This detailed instruction regarding the ordinances of this feast of remembrance was given before there was actually anything to remember. This reminds us that none of the events of that dreadful night in Egypt occurred accidentally. God was always in complete control of the salvation plan.

Separation

The first instruction given regarding the feast was the discarding of all leaven from every household. The injunction was strong and the punishment for failing to comply was severe (Exod. 12:15). This casting out of the leaven was to become forever symbolic of the casting of sin and its impurities from their lives. Israel left all leaven behind as she gathered her lumps of bread. Consider all of the other things they simultaneously left behind: bondage, idolatry, rebellion, and death that had characterized Egypt. From this point in history, God used the leaven to symbolize all that should be hastily removed from the lives of those who serve him.

This casting out of the leaven was to become forever symbolic of the casting of sin and its impurities.

Even in the New Testament we see the absence of leaven analogously representative of the purity required of Christians. In 1 Corinthians 5, Paul describes a situation of gross impurity in the church. After enjoining them to put away the evil one, delivering him to Satan, he explains the necessity of keeping the church pure using the analogy of leaven.

> Your glorying is not good. Know ye not that a little leaven leaveneth the whole lump? Purge out therefore the old leaven, that ye may be a new lump, as ye are unleavened. For even Christ, our Passover is sacrificed for us: therefore, let us keep the feast, not with old leaven, neither with the leaven of malice and wickedness; but with the unleavened bread of sincerity and truth (1 Cor. 5:6-8).

Our God is serious about casting out leaven. The one who failed to do so at each observance of the feast was cut off from Israel (Exod. 12:15). Not only was the bread to be without leaven, but no leaven was to be in the house or even seen with any Israelite in all of the quarters. As the leaven was to be totally removed from the quarters, so the spiritually impure man was to be put away from the church (1 Cor. 5:13).

When Israel left the bondage of Egypt, their lump was to be a purged and new lump. The separation was to be immediate and hastily executed. So should Christians hastily and immediately cleanse themselves from the leaven of impurity, upon finding it in their spiritual lives.

They were to remember the time when they sat down near the shores of the Red Sea and ate the flat cakes on the first day of their freedom.

Upon each yearly remembrance of the great Passover, the people of Israel were to eat unleavened bread. As they did so they were to remember the time when they sat down near the shores of the Red Sea and ate the flat cakes on the first day of their freedom. They were to reminisce and pass along to their children the story of the great deliverance and instill within their children the importance of separation from sin.

May God help parents today to remember the leaven, and work to keep their souls unleavened! The leavening agents of sin in our world today are far more enslaving and powerful than the physical coercion of the Egyptians. May we realize the dangers of this leaven of the world about us and pray to the great deliverer for his mighty arm in cleansing us constantly from it.

Salvation

The great deliverance of Israel was orchestrated by God in such a manner that no one in the camp of Israel could take credit for any portion of it. From the inextinguishable flaming bush to the parting of the Red Sea, every day had been marked with obvious supernatural occurrences. Some ten times in Exodus chapters 3 through 13, the arm, hand, or finger of God is mentioned as the instrument of deliverance. God was intentionally giving the children of Israel a mighty tale of divine deliverance to be passed along to future generations of Hebrews. Notice these words spoken by Jehovah just before inflicting the plague of locusts on the Egyptians:

> And that thou mayest tell in the ears of thy son, and of thy son's son, what things I have wrought in Egypt, and my signs which I have done among them; that ye may know that I am the Lord (Exod. 10:2).

Although God expected them to talk of his power throughout all of their days (Deut. 6:7-13), the yearly feast of unleavened bread was a time specifically set aside to remember his great salvation. God instructed the Israelites concerning the unleavened bread in Exodus 12 and then immediately followed this instruction by telling them why:

> And thou shalt show thy son in that day, saying, This is done because of that which the Lord did unto me when I came forth out of Egypt. And it shall be for a sign unto thee upon thine hand, and for a memorial between thine eyes, that the Lord's law may be in thy mouth: for with a strong hand hath the Lord brought thee out of Egypt. Thou shalt therefore keep this ordinance in his season from year to year (Exod. 13:8-10).

Do you think for a moment that because he had killed and cooked the lamb, applied the blood, cast out the leaven, and hastened out of Egypt that any Israelite credited himself with freedom from bondage? Do you suppose as he sat in the wilderness eating the flat cake on that first day of freedom that he, for a moment, thought it was his works that had freed him? Certainly not.

But do you think for a moment that he would have been sitting on the sands of the wilderness eating his flat cake in new-found freedom if he had *not* followed the instructions of God to the letter? What if he had saved back a little leaven for the journey? What if he had eaten the meat raw? What if he had applied the blood only to the posts and failed to put it on the lintel? The answer is obvious. He would have been mourning over a new-made grave with the rest of Egypt.

It is easy for us to see the wonderful outstretched arm of the Lord (Exod. 6:6) and the glaring effects of his grace toward Israel in this deliverance. Yet we cannot overlook the fact that all of his benefits were contingent upon their faithful obedience. It is obvious that neither his grace nor man's works were working exclusively. His grace was not lessened by its demands of obedience. Man's works were not excluded for fear that any would credit himself with the miraculous exodus. Such presumption would be preposterous in light of the great salvation.

No one bragged that day in the wilderness, that having applied the blood to the doorposts and lintels, he had earned his family's deliverance.

We can see this principle today. We can teach this principle to our friends who, like the vast majority of religious folks today, think that salvation requires no human activity. No one bragged that day in the wilderness, that having applied the blood to the doorposts and lintels, he had earned his family's deliverance. Yet no one would have dared leave the door unpainted, for the great mercy of God was contingent upon an obedient belief.

Baptism in water for the remission of sins is not a work of which I can boast. I cannot say that because I've complied with his conditions of pardon that I have earned his eternal deliverance. In view of the sending of his Son, such an assertion would be preposterous. But I will not escape the bondage of sin if I fail to comply with his directives, the contingencies he has placed upon my salvation.

The blood on the doorpost was the evidence of their faith. Baptism for the remission of sins (Acts 2:38) is the evidence of my faith and it is, in fact, in baptism that I access the death and blood of my Passover Lamb (Rom. 6:3-4; 1 Cor. 5:7).

Let us often stop, as we travel toward our eternal land of promise, and remember our Great Deliverer in praise and thanksgiving.

Sacrifice

It was at the time of the original passing over, that great night of destruction, that God claimed the firstborn of all man and beast for his own. The Israelites were commanded to set apart, as a sacrifice to the Lord, all males that opened the womb (Exod. 13:12-15). Exceptions were the donkeys, which were to be redeemed with a substituted lamb and, of course, their own sons which were also redeemed by a lamb. They were to take this firstborn consecration so seriously that if a man could not substitute a lamb offering for his donkey, then he was to break the neck of the donkey (Exod. 13:13).

God expected this firstborn sanctification system to create a curiosity within the children in future generations. He prepared those who witnessed the slaughter in Egypt and the miraculous exodus to use these questions to instill faith in the hand of God.

> And it shall be when thy son asketh thee in time to come, saying, What is this? that thou shalt say unto him, By strength of hand the Lord brought us out of Egypt, from the house of bondage (Exod. 13:14).

This being one of three yearly feasts of the Hebrews in which all of the males appeared before the Lord, the Passover was a time when the consecration of the firstborn symbolically reminded the entire assembly of the redemption of Israel's firstborn in that first great Passover when they applied the blood of the lamb to their houses.

The second type of sacrifice associated with the yearly Passover was the reenactment of the slaying of the lamb. This was to be done on the fourteenth day of the first month at even. In Numbers 9, there was a Passover feast in which there were some men who were defiled because they had been near a dead body. The unclean men were not even to be in the camp with God's people (Num. 5:2). Their dilemma was brought to the attention of Moses who took their question to God. How were they to participate in this holy sacrificial rite when they were unclean? God did not exclude them from keeping the Passover. Instead he gave an alternate date to be kept by anyone who found it truly impossible to keep it on the fourteenth of the first month. He enjoined on these people all of the ordinances of the original Passover (vv. 6-12). Notice verse 13 which concludes this discussion about whether the Passover sacrifice could ever be omitted:

> But the man that is clean, and is not in a journey, and forbeareth to keep the Passover, even the same soul shall be cut off from among his people: because he brought not the offering of the Lord in his appointed season, that man shall bear his sin (Num. 9:13).

Jehovah was serious about the sacrifice. This and all sacrifices were to be of the firstlings and without blemish. The sacrifices were constant reminders that it was because of the blood of the lamb, that they were released from the bondage of Egypt. What power in this symbolism for those of us who have been redeemed by Christ, our Passover! (Heb. 10:10.)

Jehovah is still serious about sacrifice. We must contact the blood of the Lamb through baptism, but the symbolism of sacrifice doesn't stop there. Romans 12:1 calls us to present ourselves as living sacrifices, holy and acceptable to him. This sacrifice is our spiritual service. If the dead sacrifices were so critical to Jehovah, surely our living sacrifices are not optional in pleasing him. Romans 12:2 completes the thought, telling us how we present ourselves unblemished as sacrifices: "And be not conformed to this world: but be ye transformed by the renewing of your mind, that ye may prove what is that good and acceptable and perfect will of God." Let us never attempt to offer to God a blemished sacrifice, spotted by the world. But let us draw near with a true heart in full assurance, "having our hearts sprinkled from an evil conscience" (Heb. 10:22).

If the dead sacrifices were so critical to Jehovah, surely our living sacrifices are not optional in pleasing him.

The Passover feast, or the feast of unleavened bread, planned by God to memorialize a deliverance yet to come, was the occasion at which the Lord's supper was to be instituted by the perfect Lamb of God. This memorial, too, was planned and instituted before the shedding of the Lamb's blood in the great Calvary deliverance. Both memorials were designed to remind the children of God of the necessary separation from sin, the great salvation afforded by the grace of God when we do cast aside the leaven of sin, and the sacrifices demanded by the God we serve.

Questions

1. There are throughout scripture many passages that draw a sharp contrast between the blessings of those who are in a covenant relationship with the Lord and the fate of those who are outside this covenant. Find and list three of these passages. Key words might be *blessing* and *curse*.
2. As the Israelite people walked through their doors never to return, describe how the lamb was above them, beside them, and in them?
3. In what ways did God show that he wanted their exodus to be done in haste? What spiritual significance might this have for us?
4. How do we know that God was in complete control of the events of the Passover night? Was the sacrifice of Christ on Calvary (our deliverance) an accident as some premillennialists claim? Did the Jews thwart the purpose of God when they killed the Christ?
5. What is symbolized by leaven? According to Deuteronomy 16:4, to what extent were the children of Israel to put away leaven for a seven-day period?
6. List other New Testament passages which refer to leaven with a negative connotation.
7. What use did God expect his people to make of a child's curiosity? Discuss ways parents can make practical application of this principle today? Discuss Deuteronomy 6:4-12 and its modern application for Christian parents.
8. How did the deliverance illustrate the "salvation by grace, faith, and works" principle? Find a New Testament passage that speaks of grace combined with faith that is obedient.
9. Find ten verses in Exodus chapters 3 through 13 that speak of the arm, the hand, or the finger of God.
10. What are some practical ways today by which Christians may demonstrate their sacrificial, separated lifestyles?
    a. How do we often fail to be separated from the world?
    b. List several New Testament passages that demand that God's people be separated from the world.

In Memory
New Testament

Lord's Supper

Matthew 26:26-29; Mark 14:22-25
Luke 22:15-20

It was Thursday evening, less than twenty-four hours before the crucifixion, when Jesus and his apostles were assembled in a quiet upper room in Jerusalem to observe the Passover. Jesus faithfully observed the Passover during his years on the earth, and this final week of his life was no exception. This feast was to be the last Passover feast to memorialize the great deliverance from Egyptian bondage. A new feast was established on this occasion to memorialize a much greater deliverance—a spiritual deliverance imminent in the death and resurrection of Christ in the days immediately to follow. It is interesting that, as we noted regarding the Passover feast, the memorial was established prior to the deliverance; the remembrance was enjoined before the actuality of the event itself. This shows us that, unlike the proponents of premillennialism would have us believe, there were no foiled plans at Calvary. The events that took place at Calvary were exactly those of which God spoke first in Genesis 3:15 and continued to promise through his prophets and through the preaching of John the Baptist. The kingdom Jesus had always intended to purchase and establish was at hand as he sat around this Passover table. In fact, he told the apostles that he would not eat of the unleavened bread or drink of the cup again until he did so in the kingdom. The kingdom of Christ is not something for which we wait today.

The Bread

The unleavened bread, as discussed in the previous chapter, had always been symbolic of the casting away of the bondage of sin. Christ gave thanks for the bread and divided it among the disciples. His words were simple: "This is my body which is given for you: this do in remembrance of me" (Luke 22:19).

I am in awe of the wisdom of our God when I think of the simplicity of this memorial. The memorial is not a statue or shrine to which I must travel. It is not observed in the possession of some corruptible item that I might lose or break. The memorial is a simple replenishable piece of unleavened bread, readily available in all areas of the world.

Every time I partake of the unleavened bread I am reminded of the malignity of sin and its disastrous consequences in my life.

The unleavened bread is symbolic of the Lord's body. While partaking of it, we're instructed simply to remember him. Having studied the original feast of unleavened bread and being aware of the symbolism of leaven enriches our partaking of the bread. Every time I partake of the unleavened bread I am reminded of the malignity of sin and its disastrous consequences in my life. I am reminded that just as the Israelites hastily cast the leaven from the bread, so I am to cast the leaven of sin from my life. I am reminded that it is only because of Christ, the only one ever to live upon the earth completely pure from the leaven of sin, becoming sin for me (2 Cor. 5:21), that I can be free from sin's power in my life. So as I partake of the unleavened bread I find myself at the foot of the cross praising him for my Passover (1 Cor. 5:7), thanking him for salvation by his grace (Tit. 2:11), praying for strength for separation from the leaven of sin, and purposing to offer myself during the coming week as a living sacrifice (Rom. 12:1-2).

The Cup

Jesus gave thanks for the cup saying: "This cup is the new covenant in my blood, which is shed for you" (Luke 22:20).

Again we are touched by this simple memorial. The cup was defined by Jesus as the "fruit of the vine," grape juice, a commodity readily available. We are simply told that it symbolizes the new covenant in his blood. Anyone, in any era of any culture, can observe this modest memorial.

Once again, inspiration draws us back to the original saving blood of the lamb so central to that first Passover. Recall it was only in the application of the blood that the firstborn of Israel were spared. Their deliverance, as ours, was borne of blood, the blood of the unblemished lamb. As I drink of the cup I am reminded of the cruel slavery of sin. I reflect on its disastrous consequences occurring all around me in the lives of those who have yet to be freed. I praise him for the blood on the doorposts of my heart.

The Pattern

Christians today assemble each Sunday to partake of the Lord's supper. This follows the only example given in Scripture which includes a reference to time: "And upon the first day of the week when the disciples came together to break bread, Paul preached unto them" (Acts 20:7).

This verse strongly implies that the purpose for which they had come together on that particular day was to partake of the Lord's supper. Since this is the only biblical reference to the time of their partaking, we can be assured that we are pleasing the Father if we partake each first day of the week.

In following the pattern of Christ, we also give thanks for the bread and the cup, respectively, before partaking of each emblem. It is important to verbalize our thanksgiving for the bread and for the cup since this is the example Jesus gave us. Long prayers are sometimes offered at the Lord's table without even a reference to the bread or cup. Jesus' purpose in praying before the breaking of bread was thanksgiving and blessing. Such should be our purpose.

Each individual Christian is charged with solemnizing within his own heart the memory of the Savior's death.

Some have adopted a practice of singing while partaking of the Lord's supper. There is no command, example, or implication for such practice—no scriptural authority. We dare not act without authority!

Further, each individual Christian is charged with solemnizing within his own heart the memory of the Savior's death. Just as each person partakes, each person is instructed to remember. Remembering is not a group effort. It is something that takes place in each heart. When I attempt to participate in the thought pattern of a song that a group is singing, I forfeit some of the control of my own thought processes.

A Matter of the Heart

By the time Paul wrote the first letter to the Corinthians, the solemn feast had been allowed to deteriorate into a common meal, seemingly characterized by gluttony and drunkenness. One can imagine how this could occur in a city like Corinth, a large commercial city which claimed notoriety for its social acceptance of sin. It was the meeting place, as it were, for all the evil and shame of other nations. All other religions of the day in Corinth were characterized by licentious practices actually committed in worship to various gods and goddesses. It became difficult for the Christians, living in the midst of a New Testament Sodom, to keep their lives and worship practices pure. We should read 1 Corinthians 11 often and allow Paul's admonitions to these brethren to strengthen our defenses against the corruption of the world around us.

It is not easy to dismiss from our minds the pollution of sin with its materialism, or just to exclude the clutter of our busy schedules when we observe the supper. I don't know how many times I've been in an assembly around the Lord's table, only to be distracted by a child's sneezing, a teenager's laughing or talking, thoughts of the class I just finished teaching, or the busy afternoon schedule ahead of me. Our thoughts are difficult to harness. And yet focus is the essence of acceptable worship. Every Christian should be as still, solemn, and reverent as possible during the Lord's supper, being careful to do nothing distractive to fellow worshipers. Parents should see that their children, even teenagers, are reverential during all acts of worship, but particularly during this communion. It is unwise for us as parents to allow our sons and daughters to sit behind us during worship, for their conduct is our responsibility. When young members of the body are passing notes, talking, laughing, and flirting during this time of special focus, they are certainly not discerning the Lord's body. They are thus eating and drinking damnation to themselves (1 Cor. 11:29). Verse 30 goes on to say that it is for this reason that many in the congregation at Corinth were weak and sickly.

It is unwise for us as parents to allow our sons and daughters to sit behind us during worship, for their conduct is our responsibility.

The heart with which we approach this feast affects the whole of our spiritual health. Let's do all we can within our own hearts to provide an atmosphere that is conducive to concentration and to remembering the blessed covenant of salvation made possible through his blood.

Another dangerous practice regarding the Lord's supper is "card-punching." I saw it first when worshiping with a congregation in which the Lord's supper was observed near the end of the worship hour. As soon as the observance was completed, a number of people sitting near the back would exit the building as if they had completed the only important item of worship. Later, while worshiping with Christians who observed the supper near the beginning of the worship, I actually witnessed a young girl hurry into the nursery during a service, say hello to her Mom, and then say, "Well, I'm going into the auditorium to take the Lord's supper." Her mom informed her that she was too late. The supper had already been passed. The girl seemed very disappointed that she had missed the communion. I guess this meant she would have to come back that night.

We are not punching a ticket to heaven simply by swallowing a piece of unleavened bread and drinking some juice!

The vehicle through which we worship when eating the Lord's supper is the heart. We are not punching a ticket to heaven simply by swallowing a piece of unleavened bread and drinking some juice! Listen to the Holy Spirit:

> For as often as ye eat this bread and drink this cup, ye do show the Lord's death till he come. Wherefore, whosoever shall eat this bread, and drink this cup of the Lord, unworthily, shall be guilty of the body and blood of the Lord. But let a man examine himself, and so let him eat of that bread, and drink of that cup. For he that eateth and drinketh unworthily, eateth and drinketh damnation to himself, not discerning the Lord's body (1 Cor. 11:26-29).

I recently heard of a church that offered a drive-through communion. Really! Those traveling out of town or rushing to keep a Sunday appointment could actually drive up to a window, hear a prayer on an intercom, and receive the emblems at their car for quick observance. In this way, their worship didn't interfere with the plans of the day at all. Surely all of us see the absurdity of this blasphemous practice. How could my heart possibly be attuned to that supreme sacrifice of Calvary, if I'm unwilling to sacrifice the pleasures of this world to pay homage to the God of my salvation by reverently assembling with the saints (Heb. 10:26), to participate in all of the commanded avenues of worship?

But aren't we guilty of a less blatant form of the same pattern of thinking when we are involved in worldly pursuits such as traveling, sports, or family gatherings during the worship hour on Sunday morning, and then partake of the supper on Sunday night? Whatever is so important to us that it draws us from the assembly on Sunday morning, has become too important. How can we expect God, who knows our hearts, to be impressed with the homage we pay to the dying Lamb on Calvary on Sunday night, when the cross and all of redemption was not important enough to bring us to worship on Sunday morning? "But let a man examine himself, and so let him eat" (1 Cor. 11:28).

Whatever is so important to us that it draws us from the assembly on Sunday morning, has become too important.

Getting Personal and Practical

The purpose of a study of the Passover of the old covenant and the Lord's supper of our new covenant should help us be more pleasing in this important act of worship. Since the attitude with which I approach this communion is directly related to my spiritual well-being (1 Cor. 11:29-30), this study can surely establish and strengthen me in my daily life. The act of partaking of the Lord's supper is an act of the heart. But the observance, if done properly, will have far reaching positive effects on the way I practice Christianity through the week.

There are some practical lessons I have learned through the years that have helped me to reverently focus while eating the Lord's supper.

- *Closing my eyes.* If I am not reading scripture, this practice helps to filter out distractions from others in the assembly who may be moving about, tending children, or who may unwittingly just catch my eye as I am trying to remember Jesus.

- *Reading the account of the crucifixion.* This is remembering. Have your Bible marked ahead at one of the Gospel accounts, so you can use the full time to reflect as you read.
- *Praying.* I'm quite certain that reflective private prayer during the Lord's supper is not a violation of Scripture, since it is, for those of us who been delivered by the blood from the consequences of sin, a form of reflection on that sacrifice. How can I but offer a prayer of thanksgiving for my purchase? How can I but pray for strength to cast from my life the leaven of sin as I eat the bread that is free from leaven? How can I but thank him for the application of the Lamb's blood on the lintels of my heart, when I drink the cup that is his blood? For the redeemed who pray through the events of all of their days, I can hardly imagine being able to remember the Savior and the cross without approaching the throne with praise and petition.
- *Counting.* That's right, counting. As I child I was privileged to sit at the feet of some great men of God. Among them were Bobby Duncan, Franklin Camp, and both Gus and Flavil Nichols. More than one of them shared this simple counting memory-handle. Because it is organized neatly, it calls the mind back into focus. It has helped me both in prayer and in observing the Lord's supper.
    1. *One Lord*—There indeed was only one who could bear my sin at Calvary. There is no remission without blood (Heb. 9:22). The blood of bulls and goats cannot take away sin (Heb. 10:4). It is only the one pure, unspotted lamb of God that can take away the sin of the world (1 Pet. 1:18-19).
    2. *Two thieves*—My Lord was crucified between two thieves. The thieves were getting what they deserved, while Christ was the propitiation for their sin and mine.
    3. *Three crosses*—The first cross was one of rebellion. The robber on this cross mocked Christ saying, "If thou be Christ, save thyself and us." He was clearly an unbeliever and died in a state of rebellion.

       The second cross was one of redemption. The thief hanging there rebuked the rebellious thief saying, "Dost thou not fear God, seeing thou art in the same condemnation? And we indeed justly; for we receive due reward of our deeds: but this man hath done nothing amiss." He even beseeched Jesus to remember him when he came into his kingdom. He obviously had been a sinner, but having confessed that to Jesus, was commended and received a promise of Paradise from the Christ.

The third cross was that of redemption, the hope of all believers.

4. *Four partings of his garment*—(John 19:23-24). Fulfilling the prophecy of Psalm 22:18, the clothing Jesus wore to the crucifixion was divided among four soldiers. The King of kings was stripped even of his common robe, first as they put a robe of purple on him to mock him, only later to strip him and nail his body to the cross.
5. *Five wounds in his body*—As I eat the unleavened bread I remember the Passover. You will recall that the Passover lamb was to be slain and eaten, but not a bone of its body was to be broken. This was a foreshadowing of the body of Christ on the cross. The custom was to break the legs of those who were hanging on the crosses on Friday afternoon, so that their deaths would be hastened and they could be removed before the Sabbath. But in fulfillment of prophecy (Ps. 34:20), his bones were not broken because he was dead already. Upon finding Christ dead, a soldier instead pierced his side, allowing blood and water to flow from his body. This accounted for the fifth wound in his body, the others being the nail wounds in his hands and feet.
6. *Six hours of suffering*—From Mark 15:25, we learn that it was the third hour of the day when they crucified Christ. From Matthew's account we learn that he died at about the ninth hour (Matt. 27:46-50). Six hours of incredible suffering, having been forsaken by a God who could not look upon the sin he bore, ended with a cry. As Jesus yielded up the ghost, the veil of the temple was torn open in the middle; there was an earthquake and even rocks were torn asunder. Graves were opened and many bodies of the righteous were raised.
7. *Seven times Christ spoke from the cross*—I can think of no more profound words in the history of the world than those spoken by the dying Christ. I have listed them for your study and reflection as you remember him.

a. "Father, forgive them; for they know not what they do" (Luke 23:34).
b. "Verily I say unto thee, today shalt thou be with me in Paradise" (Luke 23:43).
c. "Woman behold thy son . . . behold thy mother" (John 19:26-27).
d. "I thirst" (John 19:28).
e. *"Eli, Eli, lama sabachthani?"* that is to say, "My God, My God, Why hast thou forsaken me?" (Matt. 27:46).
f. "It is finished" (John 19:30).
g. "Father, into thy hands I commend my spirit" (Luke 23:46).

These are just suggestions for maintaining concentration and respect as we observe the supper of the Lord. Often I pray on Sunday morning, as I am preparing to leave for worship, that he will help me to clear from my mind the clutter of stress and scheduling and the mental pull of the things of this world, so that my worship will be to his glory. May he help us all as we pay homage to him in proclaiming his death till he comes.

Although human words or analogies can never adequately express the depth of God's love or the significance of his unspeakable gift, the following story by an unknown author stirred in me emotions of thanksgiving and a will to glorify him in worship.

Consider a modern-day parable.

The Son's Blood

The day is over and you are driving home. The radio tells about a faraway village in which three persons have died suddenly, strangely, of a flu of unknown kind and origin. It's kind of interesting.

On Sunday, coming home from church, you hear another news release. Only now it's not three villagers in some remote part of India, but thirty thousand persons in a city near to that remote village. Tonight all the major news channels carry the story.

By Monday morning mysterious death is the lead story. For it is not just India; it's Pakistan, Afghanistan, Iran. And before you know it, you're hearing this story everywhere. Medical authorities are calling it the *mystery flu*. Panic strikes. The Surgeon General is advising that once the mystery flu is contracted, it lies dormant for about a week. Four days of unbelievable pain and suffering follow; then death—certain death!

Britain closes its borders but it is too late. South Hampton. Liverpool. London. All contaminated. It's Tuesday morning when the President of the United States makes the following announcement: "Because of a national security risk, all flights to and from Europe and Asia have been canceled."

Wednesday night. You are at a church prayer meeting. Somebody runs in from the parking lot shouting, "Turn on a radio! Turn on a radio!" The church listens to a little transistor radio held to the pulpit microphone: "Two women are lying in a Long Island hospital dying from the mystery flu."

It has come to America! Within hours it seems, this thing sweeps across the country. Medical personnel—the best we have—are working around the clock. No progress reported. No antidote found. Efforts seem futile. Oregon. California. Arizona. Texas. Florida. South Carolina. Massachusetts. It's just sweeping in from the borders.

And then, all of a sudden, the news comes out. The code has been broken! The antibody has been isolated. A cure is imminent. An antidote can be made. But blood is needed: pure, uninfected blood of a very rare type. And so, sure enough, all through the Midwest, through all those channels of emergency broadcasting, everyone is being asked to "go to your hospital and have your blood analyzed. When you hear the sirens go off in your neighborhood, please make your way quickly to the hospitals."

When you and your family get down there late on that Friday night, a long line of friends and neighbors are waiting to be screened. Nurses are running about in the waiting room and patient rooms taking blood, labeling it, and handing it to couriers who whisk it down the hall to the laboratory. You patiently wait with your family to get into the hospital. Then more nurses come on duty and start working frantically among those in the parking lot.

Finishing with your family at last, the attending nurse says quietly, "Wait here in the parking lot until we've finished the test." She then hands the labeled vials to a courier and moves to the next family. You stand with your neighbors, staring into space, scared, wondering if this is the end of the world.

Suddenly a young man comes running out of the hospital screaming. He's yelling a name and waving a clipboard. What? He yells it again. Your son tugs on your jacket and says, "Daddy, he's calling me." Before you know it, they have grabbed your boy.

"Wait a minute! Hold it!"

The young man says, "It's okay. We want to make sure he doesn't have the disease. He has got the right blood type."

He leads your son away. Five tense minutes later, out come the doctors and nurses, crying and hugging one another. Some are even laughing. An old doctor walks up to you and says, "Thank your, sir. Your son's blood type is perfect. It's clean and it's pure. From it we can make the vaccine."

As the word begins to spread all over that parking lot, people are screaming and praying and laughing and crying. But then the grey-haired doctor invites you and your wife into his office where your son is lying on a gurney.

"We didn't realize that the donor would be a minor," the doctor explained. "We need—we need you to sign a consent form."

You begin to sign and then you see that the number of pints of blood to be taken is left blank. "H-h-h-how many pints?"

And that is when the old doctor's smile fades and he says, "We had no idea it would be a small child. We weren't prepared. We need it all."

"But-but—"

"You don't understand. We are talking about the world here. Please sign. We-we need it all. We need it all!"

"But can't you give him a transfusion?"

"If we had clean blood of his type, we would. Now please sign."

In numb silence you do. The doctor takes the clipboard. "I'm sorry, we-we've got to get started. People all over the world are dying."

Could you leave? Could you walk out while your son is saying, "Dad? Mom? Dad? Are you leaving me? Why are you leaving me!"

And then how would you feel the next week, when a ceremony is held to honor your son, some folks sleep through it, and some folks don't even come because they decided to go to the lake, and some folks come with a pretentious smile and just pretend to care.

Would you want to jump up and say, "My son died! Don't you even care?"

Is that how God feels? Does he say to us, "My son died! Don't you know how much I care?"

This is how much: For God so loved the world that he gave his only begotten Son, for without the shedding of blood there is no remission of sins.

Questions

1. At the institution of the Lord's supper, Christ foretold of sin in the lives of two apostles. Who were they and what sins were to follow?
2. In what three ways are we given authority for our practices in worship? Give examples from Scripture of each.
3. How can the manner in which we partake of the Lord's supper have a direct impact on the way we live our lives during the following week? What scripture substantiates this principle?
4. Suggest some practical questions I might pose to myself while examining myself as I partake of the Lord's supper.

5. Suggest some passages that are being violated by "card-punching" observers of the Lord's supper.
6. Offer additional practical suggestions for focus during observing the supper.
7. How can mothers help insure an atmosphere conducive to worship? Suggest ways that we can prepare ahead of worship time to insure that our children are not disruptive during the partaking of the supper.
8. Draw as many parallels as you can between the Passover feast and the Lord's supper.
9. Discuss the part each of the following played in the Passover and how each affects our remembrance in the Lord's supper today: separation, salvation, and sacrifice.
10. Were there ever abuses of the Passover feast similar to the abuse of the Lord's supper that we read about in 1 Corinthians 11? (Begin by looking in Isaiah chapter 1.)

On Bended Knee

Foye Watkins

If you are paying close attention while riding on a rural highway near Lewisburg, Tennessee, you will notice a winding drive with a sign boasting *Paradise* floating above it. The adoring husband of Foye Watkins appropriately named their off-the-road rural homestead *Paradise.* As queen of *Paradise,* Foye practices biblical hospitality and sets a modern example of the worthy woman.

Foye's constant mission in the Lord's work includes service in four locations in the Southeast. Teaching preschoolers—even developing classroom material—is her passion. But in recent years, she has been in great demand as a ladies' instructor. Her talent for leading class discussions brings group knowledge to the surface. Foye also supports ladies' days and is a willing speaker.

As a graduate of Alabama Christian College, Christian education held Foye's interest. Later, she led women's associate groups in two Christian schools—Boyd Buchanan and Southern Christian University.

Foye Dooley, a native of Georgia, married James Watkins in 1948, never dreaming that one day he would be preaching on national television. Their lives have been richly blessed, not only by their work, but by their four children. Their sons, Bill and Alan, are both gospel preachers. Thirteen grandchildren and six great-grandchildren are encompassed with love from these two great leaders in the cause of Christ.

Foye hesitatingly agreed to write two chapters about prayer in *We Bow Down,* claiming inexperience as an author. But her wealth of experience and her personal dependence upon prayer have proved her to be more than qualified for the task.

On Bended Knee
Old Testament

O Jehovah

Man Created to Communicate with God

How can I, a mortal of sinful flesh, approach a magnificent being who created the heavens and the earth? The psalmist said, "Let all the earth fear the Lord; let all the inhabitants of the world stand in awe of him" (Ps. 33:8).

Do you like to wear designer clothes? Gloria Vanderbilt's name is on the outside of her creations. But when God made this earth, he did not need to put his name on the outside, for no one else can create lush meadows and beautiful sunsets. What a blessing has been bestowed on me that I can talk to my maker.

According to Webster, prayer is "an earnest request; entreaty; supplication, as to God, in praise, thanksgiving, confession." Prayer is not a psychological state that just makes me feel better. It is not a crutch in time of trouble but a sincere talk with God. We were created to be his companions. When children come home from school, parents want to hear about fears, accomplishments, and friends. Communication is the glue of close relationships. What if children talked to their parents only once a week! God wants to hear his children's needs, trials, joys, and desires daily.

Approaching God

In the following passages, note man's approach to God:

- "Do not come near here; remove your sandals from your feet, for the place on which you are standing is holy ground . . . Then Moses hid his face, for he was afraid to look at God" (Exod. 3:5-6).
- "And Joshua fell on his face to the earth, and bowed down, and said to him, What has my lord to say to his servant? . . .

Remove your sandals from your feet, for the place where you are standing is holy. And Joshua did so" (Josh 5:14-15).

- "The children of Israel saw . . . the glory of the Lord upon the house, and bowed their heads with their faces to the ground upon the pavement, and worshiped" (2 Chron. 7:1-3).
- "And Ezra blessed the Lord, the great God. And all the people answered, Amen, Amen, with lifting up their hands, and they bowed their heads, and worshiped the Lord with their faces to the ground" (Neh 8:6).
- "Then Job arose, and rent his mantle, and shaved his head, and fell down upon the ground, and worshiped" (Job 1:20).
- "Then [Hezekiah] turned his face to the wall and prayed unto the Lord" (2 Kings 20:2).
- "David therefore besought God for the child; and David fasted, and went in and lay all night upon the earth" (2 Sam. 12:16).
- "O come, let us worship and bow down: let us kneel before the Lord, our Maker" (Ps. 95:6).

These verses show preparation for prayer and worship. Some fell on their faces. Others stood and raised their hands as if receiving answers to their requests. One turned and wept with his face to the wall. Some knelt, some fasted, some shaved their heads, some tore their clothes, and some bowed down. Physical action accompanied inward feelings.

Do we give God the leftovers of our focus and attention?

What preparation do we make before approaching our Father? Are we easily distracted? Do we give God the leftovers of our focus and attention?

Our hearts and minds control our actions. But our actions can prepare us to approach God's throne. The positioning of our body to be attentive and focused is not wrong; it enhances our prayers to our Father. We are constantly to have a broken, penitent, and trusting heart.

Seeking God

Abraham set up altars in Canaan and called on the name of the Lord (Gen. 12). Perhaps, since he was in a strange land, he felt a special need. God and Abram conversed as father and son: "Fear not, Abram; I am thy shield, and thy exceeding great reward." Abram said, "Lord God, what wilt thou give me, seeing I go childless?" (Gen. 15:2.) God answered abundantly, telling Abram that he would have seed as the stars of the heaven—numberless. Abram believed what God promised (Gen. 15:6). Faith is a major requirement of prayer.

Do I believe that God has the power to answer my prayers? Do I realize my need for a confidante who is all powerful? When my heart is breaking from the separation of death or divorce, when I have cried until no more tears will fall, what gives me comfort and peace? Confiding in a friend or a godly counselor helps, but nothing heals my broken heart like talking to God, who knows my needs and cares for me with a pure love. Illnesses and hardships often become the very force to bring us back to God. God said,

Illnesses and hardships often become the very force to bring us back to God.

> If my people, which are called by my name, shall humble themselves and pray and seek my face, and turn from their wicked ways, then will I hear from heaven, and will forgive their sin and will heal their land (2 Chronicles 7:14).

If there ever was a time that a land needed healing, it is now. Our schools permit cursing and blaspheming God, but we dare not use his name seriously. Maybe we have not prayed for our rulers but only criticized them. The love of God is not taught in our schools; what can we do about it? Can we beg our Father for solutions? Are we seeking God's guidance with the faith of Abraham?

Prayer in the Home

Where did you learn to pray? A friend of mine remembers her father's going out every evening, looking up, and praying to God. I remember listening, as a child, to men and women petitioning God in the small denominational church where I was taken to worship.

However, the home is the ideal place for a child to learn about God first. Godly mothers and fathers shoulder the responsibility of teaching their children to love God and seek His wisdom.

> And thou shalt love the Lord thy God with all thy heart, and with all thy soul, and with all thy might. And these words, which I command thee this

day shall be in thine heart, and thou shalt teach them diligently unto thy children, and shalt talk of them when thou sittest in thine house, and when thou walkest by the way, and when thou liest down, and when thou risest up (Deut. 6:5-7).

The mothers and fathers of old were commanded to teach their children diligently—not in a formal classroom setting, but during everyday activities from the beginning of the day until sleep fell upon them. Did God say, "If you are not too busy or when you have opportunity, teach your children"? Certainly not! There was no need for specifics to be given about how the parents were to find the time to carry out this command. Picture the men and women of old stopping to pray throughout the day, pointing out the beautiful gifts from God, telling stories of his goodness, respecting his severity. Remember, children under the Jewish law faced a severe penalty for disobeying their parents: they were stoned. If our child were at risk of being stoned, would we be more serious in teaching obedience? Can you imagine overhearing a woman like Hannah say about her three-year-old, "I just cannot do a thing with him; he won't listen to me!" Conversely, her son Samuel probably heard many prayers from his mother's lips.

When my aunts, uncles, and cousins visited my grandmother, she always called everyone together before they went home and led a solemn prayer of thanksgiving and petition for individual blessings. This routine convinced me of two things: repetition of a good thing is beneficial, and grandparents influence prayer in the home long after their own children are grown.

Repetition of a good thing is beneficial.

Teaching the love of God to children includes their learning to communicate with God. When children hear their parents pray for them and others, they imitate by using their open line to God, a line that is never busy. We owe our children this great privilege. What a joy to hear our children and grandchildren pray faithfully to God. "Children's children are the crown of old men" (Prov. 17:6). Their prayers are so simple—no showmanship or fancy words. Their words are so trusting, without guile or greed, though memorized they might be.

Most children learn rhyming prayers sitting on their mother's lap. But how much training and example are we instilling in them to make praying as regular as brushing their teeth or taking a bath? Does hygiene take precedence over prayer in the modern home? When we encourage a child to pray, we learn the meaning of "such is the kingdom of heaven." A child will pray for everything in the house and in the yard. Even when the words are all mixed up, the intent of the heart is pure. One child sincerely prayed, "Forgive us our trash passes, as we forgive those who pass trash against us."

Once a squirming, whining four-year-old boy taxed his mother's patience to the limit in worship service. She finally marched him outside the door to paddle him. As the door closed behind them, she heard his small voice, "Mama, can we kneel and pray?" One of the rewards of teaching our children is that they in turn teach us.

We need to pray daily for each child by name in his presence.

We need to pray daily for each child by name in his presence. When we are confident that God is truly on our side, our children sense our confidence and find strength in God's love. Talk with your children about how God answers prayer: sometimes "yes," sometimes "no," and sometimes "not now."

When Abraham asked if Ishmael could be his heir, God said no. He was not discouraged. His prayer life was so genuine that even his servants knew his God. When Abraham sent his servant to find a wife for Isaac from Abraham's family, he prayed a simple prayer: "O Lord God of my master Abraham, I pray thee, send me good speed this day, and show kindness unto my master Abraham" (Gen. 24:12). God answered this prayer with a yes. Then Eliezer bowed down his head and worshiped God.

How patient are we when God says, "Not now"? Abraham was promised the land of Canaan; his descendants inherited it more than four hundred years later. Our reckoning of time and God's reckoning of it are not the same. "But, beloved be not ignorant of this one thing, that one day is with the Lord as a thousand years, and a thousand years as one day" (2 Pet. 3:8). If we will stop long enough to be quiet, we will see that God is in control.

Manoah prayed upon learning that he would have a son. He said, "Teach us what we shall do unto the child that shall be born" (Judg. 13:8). Job was concerned about his children and offered sacrifices for them on a celebration day lest they had sinned (Job 1:5). How totally helpless parents are without an open door to the throne of God. In this age of hurry-scurry, we need the quiet time of family prayer and devotion. Things are temporary; our children's souls are immortal.

Personal Prayer

Solomon

Do you remember, as a child, feeling lost and overwhelmed? A child in the midst of hundreds of strangers is powerless to find his way. Solomon conveyed these feelings of bewilderment to God in this personal prayer for guidance and help:

> Thou hast showed unto David my father great mercy . . . And, now, O Lord my God, thou hast made thy servant king instead of David my father: and I am but a little child: I know not how to go out or come in, and thy servant is in the midst of thy people which thou hast chosen, a great people, that cannot be numbered nor counted for multitude. Give therefore thy servant an understanding heart to judge thy people, that I may discern between good and bad: for who is able to judge this thy so great a people? (1 Kings 3:6-9.)

What a noble prayer! He offered up thanksgiving and praise before making his plea for guidance and an understanding heart. May we pray for an understanding heart and the ability to judge wisely. James says, "If any of you lack wisdom, let him ask of God" (Jas. 1:5). From Solomon's example of personal prayer, I can make my own prayer guide.

1. Recognize God's power, love, mercy, kindness.
2. Praise his name and great qualities.
3. Admit frailty and weakness; show humility.
4. Make requests; ask for blessings.

Moses

When God told Moses to lead the Israelites out of Egyptian bondage, Moses prayed. After he had returned from Mt. Sinai and had broken the two stone tablets in anger, God said, "I will not go up [to Canaan] in the midst of thee" (Exod. 33:3). Then Moses begged of God in an "if I have, show me" prayer:

> See, thou sayest unto me, Bring up this people: and thou hast not let me know whom thou wilt send with me. Yet, thou hast said, I know thee by

> name, and thou hast found grace in my sight. Now, therefore, I pray thee, if I have found grace in thy sight, shew me now thy way, that I may know thee, that I may find grace in thy sight: consider that this nation is thy people (Exod. 33:12-13).

At times God would have destroyed Israel, but Moses reasoned with him about how it would look to the nations around them, and God listened. We can tell God exactly how we feel. He always listens.

Hannah

Hannah prayed out of bitterness of soul because she had no children and Peninnah "provoked her sore." In her sorrow, to whom did she go? Her next-door neighbor? The "Dear Abby" of the community? No, she went to the only one who could help her, her heavenly Father. She vowed a vow saying,

> O, Lord of Hosts, if thou wilt indeed look on the affliction of thine handmaid ... [and] wilt give unto thine handmaid a man child, then I will give him unto the Lord all the days of his life (1 Sam. 1:11).

Hannah's prayer was conditional: "If you will, I will." This was a prayer of commitment, faith, and humility—not a foolish vow. Her son Samuel became a great judge and prophet at a time when Israel was backsliding. He was a powerful instrument in assisting God's people with the transition from the rule of the judges to the rule of the kings.

David

David, a man of prayer, begged God for cleansing and mercy after his sin with Bathsheba:

> Have mercy on me according to thy loving kindness, according to the multitude of thy tender mercies, blot out my transgressions. Wash me thoroughly from mine iniquity, and cleanse me from my sin ... Create in me a clean heart, O God: and renew a right spirit within me . . . The sacrifices of God are a broken spirit: a broken and a contrite heart, O God, thou wilt not despise (Ps. 51:1-17).

It is quite clear that men and women in the Old Testament came with reverence and awe before their God but also with great trust that he would hear and answer.

Job

Job believed in God completely and feared him. God had blessed him in everything: children, property, and great wealth. But Satan hated for God's child to be so blessed, so he accused Job before God. God trusted Job's reaction and faith so much that he allowed Satan to try Job. Job's upright life led God to say: "Have you considered My servant Job, that there is none like him on the earth, a blameless and upright man, one who fears God and shuns evil?" (Job 1:8.)

If God said, "Have you considered my servant, Foye?" would I react as Job did? Place your name in this question. Does God consider you to be his servant, to be upright, fearing Him? God allowed Satan to kill all of Job's children and rob him of all his wealth. How did Job react?

Does God consider you to be his servant, to be upright, fearing Him?

> Then Job arose, and rent his mantle and shaved his head, and fell down and worshipped and said, "Naked came I out of my mother's womb, and naked shall I return thither: the Lord gave, and the Lord hath taken away: blessed be the name of the Lord" (Job 1:20-21).

Some of us have suffered loss due to tornadoes, floods, or natural disasters, but what about losing all your wealth and then all your children? And then, what about losing your health? No soft bed on which to lay your sick head, no car to take you to medical care, no warmth or cooling from a central unit, no nourishment to heal your diseased body, and no decent roof over your head. Would you say, "Poor me," or, "Why, why, why?" Would you talk to God about it? Do you put too much trust in material things instead of God who gave them? Do you give God the credit for your many blessings by praising him and thanking him daily?

Intercessory Prayers

The more we pray and study, the more we become interested in others. Let's observe some Old Testament examples of praying for others.

Abraham prayed for Lot and his family not to be destroyed in Sodom. God, because of Abraham, brought them out of the city before it was destroyed.

Moses prayed for the Israelites when they were about to appoint a captain and return to Egypt. Moses pled with them not to return to Egypt but they wanted to stone him. The glory of the Lord appeared in the tabernacle; the Lord said he would smite them with pestilence and make of Moses a great nation. Moses begged God not to destroy them.

> Now I beseech thee, let the power of my God be great, according as thou hast spoken, saying, The Lord is longsuffering, and of great mercy, forgiving iniquity and transgression, and by no means clearing the guilty . . . Pardon, I beseech thee, the iniquity of this people according to the greatness of thy mercy, and as thou hast forgiven this people, from Egypt until now (Num. 14:17-19).

We see why Moses was called the meekest man between Adam and Christ—he could have been the father of a great nation, but he begged for forgiveness for his people. Would you have prayed for those who were about to stone you? Is it hard for you to ask for good things for those who wrong you? What if your child has made a serious mistake and, rather than trying to help him back to God, friends gossiped? When someone spreads bad news, many times the very sin that they gossiped about visits their home. Do we feel glad when this happens? Consider this illustration:

Is it hard for you to ask for good things for those who wrong you?

> Melanie loved to be the first in the congregation to spread juicy gossip. So when she learned that Shirley had been caught shoplifting, Melanie immediately called the women in her circle at church to tell them the bad news. It took up most of her day. During the weeks following, gossiping tongues wagged. No one visited Shirley. No one prayed for her, yet her name was on many tongues. Shirley confessed her sin before the congregation, and went through counseling, never repeating her sin.
>
> A few months later, Melanie received a call from the police. Her daughter Morgan had been arrested for shoplifting! As she tearfully raced to the police station, these words kept echoing in her mind, "What goes around comes around."

Moses' wanted what was best for his people even when they had done him a terrible injustice. Can we be like Moses and pray for those who deeply wound us? You ask, "How can I pray when I do not know what to say?" God understands a pleading spirit. How often do I stop by and pray with a friend who has been unkind to me? Am I sincerely happy when good things happen to such a friend?

Prayers for Leaders

We have already seen the example of personal prayer from 1 Kings 3:6-9. As he faced the solemn responsibility of leading God's chosen people, Solomon begged of God, "Give therefore thy servant an understanding heart to judge thy people, that I may discern between good and bad: for who is able to judge this thy so great a people?" Solomon also prayed a beautiful prayer when he dedicated the temple (1 Kings 8:22-53). He prayed for all the children of Israel and even strangers who would come into the land. How wonderful it would be if our leaders really prayed for our nation.

We are supposed to pray for our leaders, but maybe we are not sincerely praying for them. What should we ask God to grant our leaders?

1. Providential care and guidance (1 Kings 3:9)
2. Wisdom (1 Kings 3:9)
3. Life (Ezra 6:10)
4. Welfare and peace for the nation (Jer. 29:7)
5. Courage (Num. 13:30; 14:24)

Let us beg God to watch over us and send us leaders who will lead us back to the right way. May God remind us that he is still in charge and sets over nations whomsoever he will (Dan. 4:25). Do I just criticize and grumble and leave God out? What do I expect if I am silent about it when I say my prayers?

Prayers for Healing

> In those days was Hezekiah sick unto death. And the prophet Isaiah, the son of Amoz came to him, and said unto him, Thus saith the Lord, Set thine house in order; for thou shalt die, and not live. Then he turned his face to the wall, and prayed unto the Lord, saying, I beseech thee, O Lord, remember now how I walked before thee in truth and with a perfect heart, and have done that which is good in thy sight. And Hezekiah wept sore (2 Kings 20:1-3).

When Hezekiah prayed for healing, God added fifteen years to his life. God said, "I heard your prayer and saw your tears" (2 Kings 20:5-6). God listens. He knows our every heartache, sees every tear, and works what is best for us. Hezekiah's prayer was answered yes. May God help us to be patient even when we do not understand why we do not always get a yes answer.

Summary

When Hannah was so burdened with sorrow over being childless, and she felt the weight of her problem was too heavy for her to bear, where could she go but to the Lord?

Job longed to hear from God because of his weariness: "My soul is weary of my life" (Job 10:1). How many of us have burdens and cannot find the answers! Job could not believe that bad things should happen to good people; but when God spoke to him, he repented in dust and ashes. Difficulty often turns us to the only one who can help us. "When my soul fainted within me, I remembered Jehovah" (Job 2:7).

Remember this: God hears you wherever you are—on the highest mountain or in the depths of the sea. Jonah prayed to God out of the belly of a fish and God heard him (Jon. 2:1-2). Whether we are rich or poor, he knows and hears our pleas. On the darkest night or the brightest day, we must pray. Remember, David said: "It was good for me that I have been afflicted; that I might learn thy statutes" (Ps. 119:71). When we search for God we will find him; affliction often initiates the search.

David also said: "Refuge failed me: no man cared for my soul" (Ps. 142:4). When we are alone and forsaken by man, God waits for our call. When our hearts are broken and no one seems to care, God listens and knows our cares. We are like little children who feel very insecure walking in a crowd, held only by Mom and Dad's fingers. Children will often extend their arms upward, wanting to be held up above the wall of knees and swinging purses, where they feel safe and secure. Isaiah reminds us that God "tends his flock like a shepherd, gathers them in his arms, and carries them close to his heart." What a comforting picture! His children cradled next to his heart. Arm's length is not close enough. He longs to draw us nearer, to protect and care for us.

"It was good for me that I have been afflicted; that I might learn thy statutes."

When life seems overwhelming, we can rest our heads next to the Father's heart, allowing him to be the gentle shepherd who comforts and protects. Can we visualize God's lifting us above the crowded street of life and pulling us close? Can we feel him gently placing his hand on our head and pressing it close to his heart? Let's allow him to be our Comforter and our Shepherd.

Before I rise to meet the day,
Before the commotion starts.
I ask you, Lord, to lift me up,
And cradle me close to your heart.
—*Power for Today*

Montague said, "Can anything be imagined so ridiculous that this miserable wretched creature, who is not so much a master of himself, but subject to the injuries of all things, should call himself master of world?" How can mortal man face daily struggles without a being wiser and stronger than himself? Prayer, to the one who controls it all, is our highway to Heaven.

Questions

1. What is prayer?
2. How should we approach God?
3. How often should we pray to God?
4. What question did Abraham ask God in Genesis 15:2?
5. Name four things in 2 Chronicles 7:14 that were necessary to heal their land.
6. List three ways that children learn to pray. What is the best way?
7. Does the command in Deuteronomy to teach our children carry over into the New Testament? If so, how are you obeying this command?
8. What servant prayed as he searched for a wife for his master's son?
9. Where did David find his help?
10. What man prayed that he would know how to treat his expected son?
11. What man prayed for wisdom to guide or judge his kingdom?
12. What is one way to obtain wisdom?
13. Who said, "Show me now thy way, that I may know thee?"
14. Who provoked Hannah?
15. Do we sin if we do not bow or kneel when we pray? Explain.
16. From Psalm 51, tell what is pleasing to God when we pray.
17. Give some attitudes that are important for successful prayer.
18. Write a sample prayer using the prayer guide from Solomon.
19. Research and report on Daniel's prayer life.

Through Christ

"And it came to pass, that, as he was praying in a certain place, when he ceased, one of his disciples said unto him, Lord, teach us to pray, as John also taught his disciples" (Luke 11:1).

Christ gave careful attention to his disciples' plea, "Teach us to pray." As a result, we have the Master Teacher's exact words of instruction at our fingertips. Additionally, the prayers offered during the entire time of the writing of the scriptures are a testimony for our benefit.

Let's examine Matthew's account of the model prayer, often called the "Lord's Prayer" but better, the "Disciples' Prayer."

> After this manner thereforepray ye: Our Father which art in Heaven, hallowed be thy name. Thy kingdom come, thy will be done on earth, as it is in heaven. Give us this day our daily bread. And forgive us our debts as we forgive our debtors, and lead us not into temptation, but deliver us from evil, for thine is the kingdom, and the power, and the glory, for ever, Amen (Matt. 6:9-13).

Our Father Which Art in Heaven

Christians can rightly address God as "our Father" because we are in his family. As a child making a request to his earthly father, there should be no fear when approaching God in prayer, but reverence and a proper relationship are essential. Revere God for who he is and build a relationship with him through conversation. Talk to God through prayer and listen to him through his word. How may I bring something worthwhile into the relationship with God? God is not served "by men's hands as though he needed anything, seeing he giveth to all life, and breath, and all things" (Acts 17:25). What can I give God that makes him happy? My love, my thanks, my praise!

A father is not in need of physical or material things from his children; the best reward he can receive from his child is grateful appreciation, demonstrated through genuine love and obedience. These qualities build a great relationship. Just as parents love children before the children love them, God loved us and gave his most precious possession for us before we loved him. I cannot repay this debt, but I can be grateful and tell God how truly great he is. All my works are but filthy rags, but a broken and contrite heart God accepts. (See Isaiah 66:2; Psalm 51:17; Psalm 34:15, 17.)

God's ears are open to our cries. As mere humans we can approach him in prayer—unworthy sinners though we are—because he is our Father. His home is Heaven, where we will live with him eternally. The apostle Paul said, "Let us come boldly unto the throne of grace, that we may obtain mercy, and find grace to help in time of need" (Heb. 4:16).

We know we are not worthless, for our Father owns the world. So why will we not trust him to care for us? If God knows the number of hairs on our head and knows when each sparrow falls to the ground, then I know he loves and cares for me.

Hallowed Be Thy Name

God's name stands for all that he is, every attribute and all the power that he possesses. The psalmist said it like this: "Holy and reverend is His name" (Ps. 111:9). We notice that the model prayer does not start as most of ours. Jesus taught his disciples to mention God first: "Hallowed be thy name." We usually begin with our wants and our needs, and if we pray long enough we will mention God's attributes and his interests. Note that the first three pleas are focused on the Father: thy name, thy kingdom, thy will.

"Come as you are" frequently glares at us from church marquis, reinforcing a cultural attitude of pleasing ourselves.

We live in a casual world; we dress down on Fridays at work. "Come as you are" frequently glares at us from church marquis, reinforcing a cultural attitude of pleasing ourselves. Does it surprise you that people have become very casual with God's name and worship? But notice that Jesus taught us, before asking anything for ourselves, God's glory and majesty is to be proclaimed.

When we approach the highest court, respect and reverence is shown.

This is a church advertisement:

> Saturday Night Live is a church service given for different folks, in a different way, at a different time . . . The time is better for many, the dress is casual. (I've seen people come straight from the garden with T-shirt and shorts), but you can dress the way you wish . . . Someone said, "They should issue seat belts for that service." This is the place where . . . one sometimes sings, "God's open for business . . . It's Saturday Night."

A recent report told of a person who approached God as, "Good morning, Daddy." Is there really an attempt in our society to humanize God, to bring him to our level so we can love him at our convenience and perceive him as an equal? Historically, men have not been able to do that. Moses at the burning bush was told, "Draw not nigh . . . Take off your shoes . . . You are on holy ground." Moses reverentially complied. He knew he was in the presence of one far greater than he.

"Holy, holy, holy, is Jehovah of hosts: the whole earth is full of his glory."

Have we really understood the full meaning of reverence? Do not forget that *awe* and *fear* and *terrify* are all inherent in reverence! Whatever these three words mean to you, I'm sure they have no commonness with *casual*.

Note Isaiah's reaction to a vision of Jehovah's sitting on his throne:

> I saw the Lord sitting on a throne . . . above him stood the seraphim . . . and one cried to another, and said, Holy, holy, holy, is Jehovah of hosts: the whole earth is full of his glory . . . Then said I, Woe is me! . . . for mine eyes have seen the King, Jehovah of hosts (Isa. 6:1-5).

How did Isaiah feel as he observed Jehovah and his seraphim? Prideful? Boastful? Casual? This great prophet of God felt unworthy in the presence of the maker of this world. Let's learn to fear and reverence God's name as Moses, Isaiah, and others did—men who came face to face with the fact that God is, indeed, the Lord of hosts. Hugh McLellan says, "Prayer is the soul drawing near to God, and when the soul draws near to God, the ground beneath our feet becomes holy ground, and the most common bush is flaming with the presence of Jehovah."

Thy Kingdom Come

Our Lord knew that he was to give his life for the eternal kingdom, his church, his bride. The kingdom was yet to come when Christ was teaching them to pray. Jesus later gave Peter the keys of the kingdom (Matt. 16:19), empowering him to preach the first gospel sermon. This sermon resulted in the establishment of the kingdom of Christ—his church, his body (Acts 2; Col. 1:18).

Christians today pray for the kingdom, but not that it will come.

Christians today pray for the kingdom, but not that it will come. It is now in existence. The Bible clearly teaches that the kingdom began in the days of the apostles. The apostle John said he was in the kingdom: "I, John, who also am your brother, and companion in tribulation, and in the kingdom and patience of Jesus" (Rev. 1:9). In the book of Hebrews, the writer also mentions the kingdom: "But of the Son he saith, Thy throne, O God, is forever and ever" (Heb. 1:8). It is said to be the kingdom of Christ and God (Eph. 5:5).

So today, Christians pray for the growth of the kingdom and the faithfulness of its citizens. We pray for laborers in the kingdom. Jesus said to his disciples, "The harvest truly is plenteous, but the laborers are few; pray ye therefore the lord of the harvest, that he will send forth laborers into his harvest" (Matt. 9:37-38). We pray for elders, preachers, deacons, and teachers that assist in fulfilling this prayer.

Thy Will Be Done, as in Heaven, so on Earth

Jesus came to this earth to fulfill his Father's will: "For I am come down from heaven, not to do mine own will, but the will of him that sent me " (John 6:38). His entire life was characterized by this disposition. When John hesitated at Jesus' request for baptism—feeling that Jesus should baptize him—Jesus answered, "Suffer it to be so now; for thus it becometh us to fulfill all righteousness" (Matt. 3:15). Jesus was to do his Father's will, not his own. In the Garden of Gethsemane he prayed, "My Father, if it be possible let this cup pass away from me: nevertheless not as I will, but as thou wilt" (Matt. 26:39).

If we learn God's will through study, and then do his will, we are in position to pray to our Father with confidence. Jesus said, "For whosoever shall do the will of my Father who is in heaven, he is my brother, and sister, and mother" (Matt. 12:50). Prayer should not be an effort to change God's will, but to bring our will into harmony with his.

Give Us this Day Our Daily Bread

This plea is the first of four petitions concerning the dependence of man on God for personal needs. We are frail creatures in need of God's assistance. Bread is necessary for our physical health just as spiritual food is necessary for our soul. The same God who fed the children of Israel in the wilderness is still concerned with our physical lives today.

"Give us this day our daily bread." In other words, one day at a time is sufficient (Matt. 6:34). Tomorrow we will talk to him again. And that is what God wants. He wants us to talk to Him daily—not weekly or monthly, but daily. Through this our daily bread and our spiritual food are supplied. Even though God provides our necessities, we still must work for them (2 Thess. 3:10-12; 1 Thess. 4:10-12). He gives us the opportunity and strength to work and to provide for our families, and since God is in control, we should not be overly worried or distressed. "Therefore I say unto you, be not anxious for your life, what ye shall eat, or what ye shall drink; nor yet for your body, what ye shall put on" (Matt. 6:25).

> ***Since God is in control, we should not be overly worried or distressed.***

Yet these are things that worry most of us. Paul wrote, "In nothing be anxious: but in everything, by prayer and supplication with thanksgiving let your requests be known unto God" (Phil. 4:6). If we do this the "peace of God, which passeth all understanding, shall guard your hearts and thoughts in Christ Jesus" (Phil. 4:7). The peace of God will put a guard around your heart saying, "No external force can destroy the peace that abides here." James says, "Ye have not because ye ask not" (Jas. 4:2). "My God shall supply every need of yours according to his riches in glory in Christ Jesus" (Phil. 4:19).

Forgive Our Debts

Debts here is used instead of *trespasses,* as you will see in verses 14-15. When we seek forgiveness of our sins we must be sure we have forgiven those who sin against us, for Jesus said, "And whensoever ye stand praying, forgive, if ye have ought against anyone that your Father also who is in heaven may forgive you your trespasses" (Mark 11:25). There is not a person who is sinless and does not need forgiveness (1 John 1:8-10). When we do sin "we have an advocate with the father, Jesus Christ the righteous" (1 John 2:1). When we pray we should be conscious of the fact that our Lord Jesus Christ is making intercession for us. Have you considered what a Savior we have? He will never leave us, nor forsake us.

> Who shall separate us from the love of Christ? Shall tribulation, or distress, or persecution, or famine, or nakedness, or peril, or sword? . . . Nay, in all these things we are more than conquerors through him that loved us (Rom. 8:35-37).

As We Forgive Our Debtors

It is extremely important that we forgive others in order for Christ to forgive us. He states it again in Matthew 6:14-15: "For if ye forgive men their trespasses, your heavenly Father will also forgive you: but if ye forgive not men their trespasses, neither will your Father forgive your trespasses." This is plain enough, but he states it another way. He says that if we have a brother who has "aught against us, we must first he reconciled to him and then bring our offering" (Matt. 5:23-24). Also Matthew 18:15-35 tells of the forgiving king and the unforgiving servant. God will not forgive anyone unless that person has a forgiving heart, even praying for those who use him despitefully (Luke 6:27-35).

God will not forgive anyone unless that person has a forgiving heart.

Lead Us Not into Temptation

Does God tempt us? James says, "Let no man say when he is tempted, I am tempted of God; for God cannot be tempted with evil, neither tempteth he any man: but every man is tempted, when he is drawn away of his own lust, and enticed" (Jas. 1:13-14). Since God does not entice his children to sin, the plea not to lead us into temptation must then be asking God to protect us from unfair temptation. This thought is given by Paul:

> There hath no temptation taken you but such as is common to man: but God is faithful, who will not suffer you to be tempted above that ye are able; but will with the temptation also make a way to escape, that ye may be able to bear it (1 Cor. 10:13).

Further, James says:

> My brethren, count it all joy when ye fall into divers temptations; knowing this, that the trying of your faith worketh patience. But let patience have her perfect work, that ye may be perfect and entire, wanting nothing (Jas. 1:2-4).

Satan will tempt us through all the avenues available: the lust of the flesh, the lust of the eyes, and the pride of life (1 John 2: 16).

Deliver Us from Evil

A most accurate translation of this phrase is, "Deliver us from the evil one." Our adversary waits for us daily and knows our weaknesses. But so does our Father; he is as close as we allow. Sin, the finished product of the devil, is the wedge that separates us from God. Temptation is not sin, but we pray for God to help us avoid temptation because we realize that it leads to sin. Satan is a formidable terrorist in disguise, always ready to strike us down. Deliverance begins with the seeking of knowledge. When we know our enemy and our Saviour, it is easy to choose whom to follow!

Satan is a formidable terrorist in disguise, always ready to strike us down.

> Trust in the Lord with all your heart and lean not on your own understanding; in all your ways acknowledge Him, and He will direct your paths. Be not wise in your own eyes; revere the Lord and depart from evil; it will be healing to your body and nourishment to your bones (Prov. 3:5-7).

For Thine Is the Kingdom, and the Power, and the Glory Forever

As this model prayer began with recognition of God, so it concludes with these three incontestable facts. When a Christian fails to recognize God's everlasting power, he is clearly in violation of the principle here. In this model of communication between the heavenly Father and his child, these last words serve to exalt God and remind man of his frailty.

Guide for Prayer

We compiled a guide for prayer from Solomon in the previous chapter. Now from this model prayer, we can make another guide—this time from Christ's example.

1. Exalt God as Father.
2. Express reverence.
3. Petition kingdom maintenance.
4. Submit to God's will.
5. Depend on God daily.
6. Beg for conditional forgiveness.
7. Forgive others.
8. Avoid temptation.
9. Flee from Satan.
10. Recognize that God is in charge.

"I just don't know what to say when I pray," say many Christian women who want to talk to their Father. "What should I pray for?" These questions are answered for us above. Even a short petition including one or two of the items above is a good place to begin. Practice wording a prayer of just a few sentences. Write it down. Then expand your thoughts and write another one. Soon you will be in the habit of remembering the guide from Christ himself, and you will gain confidence, knowing that you are following the Master.

Practice wording a prayer of just a few sentences. Write it down.

Here is a prayer sample.

> Heavenly Father, you are the most holy and righteous God. I feel humbled to be in your presence. I am weak compared to you. O God, I need your mercy, and beg your help in my fight with Satan. I am thankful that you are my Father, close by to protect me from the devil. Please forgive me for my failure to obey you fully today. Thank you for blessing me with every comfort. I ask you to bless the church with strong leaders. Help me to be kind and forgiving to my family. You are the greatest power that I know; I am happy to be your child. In Christ's name, Amen.

Hindrances to our Prayers

Sin

> Out of the heart of men, proceed evil thoughts, adulteries, fornications, murders, thefts, covetousness, wickedness, deceit, lasciviousness, an evil eye, blasphemy, pride, foolishness, all these things come from within, and defile the man (Mark 7:21-23).

The heart of man must be clean and open to God's instruction, but with Satan working day and night, we must be vigilant and put on the whole armor of God so we can withstand the evil one.

> Beloved, if our heart condemn us not, we have boldness toward God; and whatsoever we ask we receive of him, because we keep his commandments and do the things that are pleasing in his sight (1 John 3:21-22).

Unbelief

> But let him ask in faith, nothing doubting: for he that doubteth is like the surge of the sea driven by the wind and tossed. For let not that man think that he shall receive anything of the Lord: a doubleminded man, is unstable in all his ways (Jas. 1:6-8).

We must have faith—no doubts—when we pray.

"Without faith it is impossible to be well-pleasing unto Him; for he that cometh to God must believe that He is, and that He is a rewarder of them that seek Him" (Heb. 11:6). Read the verse again, emphasizing the words *impossible* and *must*. There is no room for "maybe" with God.

If I can truly call God my Father from a heart that trusts, all my doubts about God's ability to hear and answer prayer will vanish, for he has said, "I will in no wise fail thee, neither will I in any wise forsake thee" (Heb 13:5).

Pride

"God resisteth the proud, but giveth grace to the humble" (Jas. 4:6). In Luke 18 two men went up to pray, one a Pharisee, and one a publican. The Pharisee was filled with pride and thought himself to be better than others. The publican "would not lift up so much as his eyes unto heaven, but smote his breast, saying, God be merciful to me, a sinner." Pride kept the Pharisee from being justified. Humility is always required for justification.

Selfishness

"Ye ask, and receive not, because ye ask amiss, that you may spend it in your pleasures" (Jas. 4:3). All of us have to fight selfishness, for we are born that way. A baby does not care how much sleep the mother loses or why he cannot have all the toys for himself. Unselfishness is a difficult lesson to learn. Parents must train their children through instruction and example.

An Unforgiving Spirit

"But if ye forgive not men their trespasses, neither will your Father forgive your trespasses" (Matt. 6:15).

Denial

"He that turneth away his ear from hearing the law, even his prayer is an abomination" (Prov. 28:9). We should divest ourselves of all malice, hatred, and bad thoughts toward others and come to God with a clear heart. God will help us to overcome the negative attributes of which we must rid ourselves.

When my day is too busy for conversation with God, am I denying him? In our age of modern technology, we can choose the sound that comes into our living room, den, bedroom, kitchen, car, and office. How many of us choose to turn it all off and talk to our Father? Are we listening to the latest hit recording on the radio, rather than seeking peace through prayer? One godly woman has to commute one hour each day to work. She uses this time alone in her car to pray for her family, herself, and those who have asked for her prayers. Do we seek time for prayer, or make excuses to deny God this fellowship?

Are we listening to the latest hit recording on the radio, rather than seeking peace through prayer?

Summary

Jesus made no secret of the importance of prayer (Matt. 14:23; Mark 6:41; Luke 6:12; 9:28-29; John 1:41-42; 17:1-26). He prayed early in the morning, all night, before eating, and before great decisions in his life. He prayed in distress of soul; he prayed as he was dying for us.

When the apostles received the miraculous power by the Holy Spirit, they still used prayer effectively. When Peter was cast into prison, the Christians met at Mary's house and prayed (Acts 12:3-17). In almost all of Paul's epistles he mentioned praying for the Christians to whom he was writing. He and Silas had their bands loosed as they were praying (Acts 16:25-30). The early church believed much in prayer (Acts 1:14). Most of us will admit that in times of great crises we have prayed anxious, fervent, and tearful prayers. When some great responsibility weighs heavily upon us, or when sorrows engulf us and loneliness leaves us in despair, we turn to God in prayer for answers. Is this the way God wants us to be? Christ prayed when he was about to be arrested and tried. This was a time of great agony and he prayed three times, "Let this cup pass from me: nevertheless, not as I will, but as thou wilt" (Matt. 26:38-44). His soul was exceedingly sorrowful, even unto death. If he needed to talk to his Father, how much more do we who are frail human beings? We must have a submissive will, just as Christ did: "Not my will, but thine be done."

The church prayed diligently when Peter was kept in prison by Herod (Acts 12:5). God released him. Paul prayed for his thorn in the flesh to be removed. God did not see fit to grant the petition but gave him the grace to endure it, for "God's strength is made perfect in weakness" (2 Cor. 12:7-9).

1. We all stand in need of prayer: "For all have sinned, and come short of the glory of God" (Rom. 3:23).
2. We "have not because we ask not" (Jas. 4:2). Why should we be hungry in a land filled with plenty? We enjoy many blessings without asking: air, water, and life. These are great but do not compare to our spiritual blessings.
3. God's ears are always open (Ps. 116:2; 1 Pet. 3:12); he never sleeps.
4. Jesus is our mediator. He pleads for us because he shed his blood as a sacrifice.

Questions
(Give the scripture reference)

1. What caused the disciples to ask Jesus to teach them to pray?
2. How do we know John the Baptist taught his disciples to pray?

3. What should be the name of the prayer, commonly called the "Lord's Prayer," that Jesus taught his disciples to pray? Why?
4. If God does not need man's hands to serve him, why does he require service of us?
5. What kind of heart will God accept?
6. Discuss the need of a child of God to come "boldly to the throne of grace."
7. How do faith and answered prayer relate?
8. Which scripture says that "God will not fail or forsake us"?
9. Name some ways we show reverence to God.
10. How should we start our prayers to God?
11. What does "hallowed be thy name" mean?
12. Discuss God's majesty. Why should we recognize his majesty as we pray?
13. How does the nature of God discourage his followers from approaching him casually?
14. What did Moses have to do when God appeared in the burning bush?
15. Discuss the significance of "thy kingdom come" as it related to Jesus' contemporaries and to us today.
16. How did Jesus prove that he came to do the will of his Father?
17. How can we know God's will for us?
18. Should prayer be an attempt to change God's will? Defend your answer.
19. What things should we pray for?
20. Why do you suppose Jesus did not teach his disciples to say, "Give us this year our yearly bread"?
21. Why did Jesus discourage his people from being anxious about tomorrow?
22. How is God's forgiveness of us tied to our forgiveness of others?
23. What does God promise us in regard to our temptations?
24. Why pray, "Lead us not into temptation"?
25. Name some hindrances to prayer.
26. How has Jesus' openness in prayer affected you?
27. Name some occasions upon which the early church prayed.
28. How should a righteous man feel about his need to pray for forgiveness?
29. How should God's "busy schedule" affect our petitions to him?

Thus Saith the Lord

Sheila Butt

A native of Rockford, Illinois, Sheila Keckler Butt holds a B.S. degree in English and History from East Tennessee State University. She is a graduate of the Women's Program of Bear Valley School of Biblical Studies. She did graduate work in Greek and Hermeneutics at David Lipscomb University.

Sheila's experiences in teaching young children and women of all ages make her a popular choice as a speaker for ladies' days, lectureships, and seminars. Teenage girls in the Horizons program at Freed-Hardeman University have, over the last twelve years, benefited from her instruction. Sheila has spoken to women at the Caribbean lectureship for five years; her travels abroad also include Jamaica, Panama, and Honduras.

No Greater Joy proved Sheila's success as an author. The book admonishes parents to nurture and train their children to love the Lord; one chapter is devoted to the husband-wife relationship in Christ. Her recently published book, *Seeking Spiritual Beauty,* is in great demand.

Sheila and her husband Stan share their secrets of a thirty-year, secure marriage, along with their experiences in parenting three sons—who are now gospel preachers with families of their own—by frequently conducting their seminar, "No Drums . . . No Bugles: The Making of a Christian Family." Sheila also excels in lecturing periodically for "In His Image," an all-girls youth rally.

Stan and Sheila reside in Columbia, Tennessee, where she always has time for their three grandchildren.

Thus Saith the Lord
Old Testament

Prophesying

Biblical teaching originates with God. The only person who ever came into the world knowing the will of God was Christ. The rest of humanity had to be taught.

In the Old Testament, God instructed the patriarchs, the prophets, and other wise men whom he had chosen to teach others. Often the teachers themselves had to be taught some very profound and personal lessons before they were capable of teaching others. When Christ entered the world, he became the mouthpiece of God. He was God incarnate, the ultimate teacher.

Jesus assures us that what he taught was from God.

> If God were your father, ye would love me; for I proceeded forth and came from God; neither came I of myself, but he sent me . . . He that is of God heareth God's words; ye therefore hear them not, because ye are not of God . . . Verily, verily, I say unto you, If a man keep my saying, he shall never see death (John 8:42-51).

In studying the preaching and teaching found in the Old and the New Testaments, one can conclude that both were intended to *inform*, to *reform,* and to *transform* the lives of human beings.

What is desperately needed today are men and women and boys and girls of courage, who will believe and obey the teachings of God regardless of what others are doing and regardless of their personal preference for the style in which the gospel is presented. We have become too accustomed to being comfortable with our preaching and our Bible classes. In our comfort zone, it is almost impossible for the gospel to change lives. At a time when some are using the *Andy Griffith Show* to teach timeless biblical truths, something has gone awry. Entertainment has replaced knowledge and truth. Comfort and personal satisfaction have replaced a contrite spirit. The ability of the word to transform lives is severely diluted by the introduction of entertainment as a method of teaching and preaching! It makes us too comfortable.

The Israelites introduced entertainment while Moses was on Mount Sinai receiving the *Ten Commandments*. We are told, "They rose up early on the morrow, and offered burnt offerings, and brought peace offerings [to the golden calf]; and the people sat down to eat and drink, and rose up to play" (Exod. 32:6). They were in their comfort zone. They were worshiping in their own way. And we are told by God in Exodus 32 that they had corrupted themselves! When we stray from God's teaching, we corrupt ourselves. We are compelled to see that in both the Old and the New Testaments God has instituted teaching and preaching as avenues for transforming lives since the beginning of time.

Old Testament Teaching

In the Old Testament, God's first instructions were given to Adam and Eve. He plainly and simply informed them—commanded them—not to eat of the fruit of the tree "which is in the midst of the garden" (Gen. 3:3). He also informed them of the consequences. At this point, there was no need for teaching or instruction which could reform or transform their lives. Adam and Eve were created by God. In the beginning, they did not need reforming or transforming. Adam and Eve were given the opportunity to lead sinless lives.

There was no paraphrasing, rephrasing, or restating in order to make Adam and Eve feel more comfortable about his instruction.

Adam and Eve, however, were also given the ability to make choices. Because they disobeyed God's instruction, there was immediate and lasting punishment. God intended for his instructions to be obeyed. There was no paraphrasing, rephrasing, or restating in order to make Adam and Eve feel more comfortable about his instruction. God simply gave his instruction and intended for the hearers to obey.

Much of our instruction, teaching, and preaching today would be more powerful if the things being taught were simply the words of God rather than the thoughts and opinions of an entire Bible class being facilitated by someone standing up in front of them.

Many of our Bible classes today look more like support group meetings than the people of God in the Old Testament who often stood in reverence and awe while the word of God was being taught or read.

Beginning in Genesis 6, we learn that "God saw the wickedness of men was great in the earth, and that every imagination of the thoughts of his heart was only evil continually. And it repented the Lord that he had made man on the earth." Obviously, God was sorry that he had made man because of man's choice not to follow his teaching and instruction. But thankfully, "Noah found grace in the eyes of the Lord" (Gen. 6:8). In 2 Peter 2:5 we are told that Noah was a preacher of righteousness, and in Hebrews 11:7 we read that Noah prepared the ark by faith, "being warned of God of things not seen as yet." Noah believed God. He followed God's teaching and instruction and it was accounted to him for righteousness.

Noah's teaching obviously got proper results even though not one of his words is recorded. In a pagan, polygamous time he had one wife and his three sons had only one wife each. Apparently Noah's instruction to his family reformed them, in other words, kept them from the pollution of the world and transformed them into people who also loved God. God was granting them salvation because they were obeying his commands. Noah's actions tell us that he obeyed God and that he had the ability to teach others.

"Well, Noah could have told the people anything just to get them to come into the ark!"

A couple of years ago when I was teaching the ladies in Jamaica about the love of God and the importance of obedience to him, a young lady who was a school teacher and a babe in Christ spoke up and said, "Well, Noah could have told the people anything just to get them to come into the ark!" How convenient that would have been. Noah could have rationalized and thought, "If I offer them a free meal or have a party, or invite a special speaker for one of society's ills, perhaps I could get hundreds of people on the boat before the flood." Truthfully, perhaps Noah could have gotten more people on the boat. But that is not what God told him to preach! And he would not have saved their souls just by saving them from the flood! God's instructions are not a quick fix.

Obedience to God comes from the heart and the result is a way of life.

God gave Noah instructions on building the ark in order that he and his family would be saved. Noah's three sons, their wives, and Noah's wife were going by faith into the ark which had been built exactly as the Lord had instructed. (Surely Mrs. Noah would have preferred some interior or exterior decorating changes, or at least some other accommodations for the animals, but Noah followed God's commands explicitly.)

It is interesting yet sad that there was not another soul in the world who listened to Noah's preaching. Maybe his style was distasteful; no one wanted to hear about the end of the world. Maybe his accent was not easy on the ears. Perhaps he got too emotional, or not emotional enough. Maybe he was too preachy. But maybe, just maybe, the reason no one else was saved had nothing to do with Noah's style of preaching, his mannerisms, or his personality. The teaching was available to everyone. The truth was being taught. But it fell on deaf ears. Noah's sinful and adulterous generation may have been lost simply because it was not listening.

We know that Abraham must have been an effective and faithful teacher because God paid him the ultimate compliment in Genesis 18:19. God said,

> For I know him, that he will command his children and his household after him, and they shall keep the way of the Lord; to do justice and judgment; that the Lord may bring upon Abraham that which he hath spoken of him.

What a wonderful tribute from God!

Moses, on the other hand, was reluctant to become a teacher. In Exodus 4:10, we see Moses entreating God to use someone else as his mouthpiece. "Lord, O my Lord, I am not eloquent, neither heretofore, nor since thou hast spoken unto thy servant; but I am slow of speech and of a slow tongue." (In other words, I was not a very good speaker before I talked with you and I have not become eloquent since you have spoken to me, either!)

> And the Lord said unto him, Who hath made man's mouth or who maketh the dumb, or deaf, or the seeing or the blind? Have not I the Lord? Now therefore go, and I will be thy mouth, and teach thee what thou shalt say (Exod. 4:11-12).

In all likelihood, Moses was very capable of preaching and teaching. We learn from Stephen in Acts 7:22 that "Moses was learned in all the wisdom of the Egyptians, and was mighty in words and deeds." Moses had the ability but lacked either the desire or the confidence to speak for the Lord. (We know, too, that zeal without knowledge does not qualify one to teach for the Lord—Romans 10:2). God assured Moses that he would be Moses' mouth.

God is still the mouth of preachers and teachers of the gospel today who use his word as the foundation and the conclusion of their teaching. Unfortunately, as Charles Hodge penned a few years ago, "Some of us have become so open minded that our brains have fallen out!" Consequently, many are unable to come to any conclusion as to what God's word says.

"Some of us have become so open minded that our brains have fallen out!"

Old Testament teaching and instruction were neither ambiguous nor did they serve as a springboard for the people of God to draw their own conclusions. The teaching and directions of Moses were the words of God. The *Ten Commandments* were not up for discussion, revision, or general consensus. God, through Moses, was not playing "Let's Make a Deal."

Moses instructed the people to do what God commanded of them. In Deuteronomy, near the end of Moses' life, he commanded Israel to "love the Lord thy God, to walk in his ways, and to keep his statutes and his judgments, that thou mayest live and multiply" (Deut. 30:16). He went on to assure them that if they did not do these things, they would perish. This teaching applied to their physical as well as their spiritual lives. Moses taught the people God; nothing more, nothing less.

Are our Bible class teachers, elders, and preachers doing that today, or are most of our classrooms filled with discussion, tolerance, and acceptance of every class member's opinion with a scripture thrown in occasionally, often out of context, just so we can call it a Bible class? Are our pulpits full of preachers who have style, charisma, and a short story to tell—certainly not more than twenty minutes—but who lack the strength, courage, and perhaps even the knowledge of the doctrine of Christ? Studies have shown that many of the denominational seminaries are filled with students who do not even believe there is a hell!

Certainly no one in the twenty-first century believes that Moses could have kept his preaching job or his class responsibilities for very long. Most congregations of Christians today would have labeled him too dogmatic and legalistic. The fact remains, however, that God's promises are conditional. They always have been. I have heard one of our contemporary preachers, Mike Tenaro, say it like this on several occasions, "Faith is believing that God will do what he says he will do, when you do what he asks you to do." The righteousness of the people in the Old Testament was based on that same faith.

We know from Romans 15:4 that "whatsoever things were written aforetime were written for our learning, that we through patience and comfort of the scriptures might have hope." The Old Testament gives us countless examples of the faithful and the unfaithful—those who followed the teaching of God and those who did not.

We consider Hebrews 11 to be the "Roll Call of the Faithful." It is literally the roll call of those who did what God told them to do. Beginning with Abel and ending with the prophets, it gives examples of those who did what God asked them to do. The chapter ends by saying that all of these obtained a good report through faith—faith that believed God would do what he said he would do, if they did what he asked them to do. They followed his teaching and instruction.

Before we consider the role of the prophets, we want to understand the responsibilities of the priests in preaching and teaching in the Old Testament. The priests were to teach the people the law of God. In Deuteronomy 9, we are told that Moses delivered the law of God to the priests. The priests were to deliver the law to the people and read it in their hearing. In Malachi we read, "For the priest's lips should keep knowledge, and they should seek the law at his mouth; for he is the messenger of the Lord of hosts" (Mal. 2:7). The priests handed down the law, which had originated from God. Ultimately that law, interpreted and adjusted, became the traditions of men.

Obviously the prophets were needed because the original function of preaching and teaching God's word which had been handed down to the priests had become distorted.

The priesthood was hereditary and the position was held for life unless a man suffered a blemish (physical disability) which would have made him unfit to come "nigh to the altar; because he hath a blemish; that he profane not my sanctuaries: for I the Lord do sanctify them" (Lev. 21:16-24).

The prophets believed that the priests of their day lacked knowledge (Hos. 4:6). Jeremiah accused them of not knowing the Lord (Jer. 2:8). Micah indicted the priests for teaching for money (Mic. 3:11). Obviously the prophets were needed because the original function of preaching and teaching God's word which had been handed down to the priests had become distorted.

In contrast to the priesthood, the prophets were not chosen by heredity. What they spoke were not the traditions which had evolved through the priesthood, but revelations from God. The Greek word for prophet, *prophetes*, means "one who proclaims a message in behalf of another." An excellent example of a prophet is Aaron; God told Moses that Aaron would be his mouth. Aaron would receive the words from Moses and speak them to the Pharaoh. The prophet, then, is the man who receives his words from God and then speaks them to the people. The words which the prophet speaks are not his own. Unlike the priests who passed the law from generation to generation, the prophets received their words directly from God through the Holy Spirit and spoke those actual words.

God used men from every walk of life and of every disposition as prophets. A man did not choose to become a prophet. He was equipped by God and God told him what to do and say. In 2 Peter 1:20-21 we read, "Knowing this first, that no prophecy of the scripture is of any private interpretation. For the prophecy came not in old time by the will of man: but holy men of God spake as they were moved by the Holy Spirit." Moses was the only prophet who had spoken to God face to face, and we are told that "there arose not a prophet since in Israel, like unto Moses, whom the Lord knew face to face" (Deut. 34:10).

God has no grandchildren, therefore the church is never more than a generation away from apostasy.

After the death of Moses, Joshua became a strong leader who continued to inspire the Israelites to serve God. We know that "Israel served the Lord all the days of Joshua, and all the days of the elders that overlived Joshua, and which had known all the works of the Lord, that he had done for Israel" (Josh. 24:31). Joshua continued admonishing the people to fear the Lord and could say without reservation, "But as for me and my house, we will serve the Lord" (Josh. 24:15).

Joshua's teaching was straightforward and enduring. However, we learn from subsequent books of the Old Testament that after the elders died who had outlived Joshua, Israel forgot—did not remember and did not practice—the instruction they had been given from God through Joshua.

God has no grandchildren, therefore the church is never more than a generation away from apostasy. Every generation has to be taught the oracles of God. Throughout the Old Testament, the further removed the people became from one of God's mouthpieces, the further removed they became from God.

In Judges 2:10-13 we see God's people begin to serve Baal and we are told that they forsook the God of their fathers. The term *spiritual adultery* is not one that we hear much anymore, but the fact is that when God's people forgot his teaching and instruction in the Old Testament and began worshiping idols, images, and false Gods, he accused them of "playing the harlot."

Over and over again in the Old Testament, God's people forgot the teaching and instruction of the Lord and left him. When they realized the consequences of disobeying God, they cried to him and God pitied them. God truly loved them. But like many of us, they wanted to behold and to indulge in the goodness of God without understanding or considering his severity (Rom. 11:22).

Many times the prophets were concerned with problems of worship. In 1 Samuel 2:27-36 we see a man of God coming to Eli and condemning Eli's household for their sacrilege and immorality. Eli was accused of honoring his own sons before God. In 1 Samuel 3:11-18 the Lord told Samuel that he would carry out his judgment of Eli's house and Samuel told Eli of his vision.

Samuel was also convinced that obedience was better than sacrifice, which had been the cornerstone of the Israelite tradition. In 1 Samuel 15:22, Samuel tells Saul, "Behold, to obey is better than sacrifice, and to hearken better than the fat of rams." In Hosea 6:6 we read, "For I desired mercy and not sacrifice: and the knowledge of God more than burnt offerings." The prophets denounced the worship of other gods, the importation of foreign elements into worship, and vain worship. They understood that obedience was more important than sacrifices. They understood that the heart of a man was more important than the traditions of men. They often addressed the sins of society.

Having been exposed to the traditions of Israel's past and understanding the great things the Lord had done, the prophets had an important message for their day. They saw the strict covenant with God being violated and they sounded warnings of judgment to be faced. The prophets called on their contemporaries for repentance even though their attempts were often in vain. They also looked beyond that judgment to a new covenant. In Micah 5:2 we read,

> But thou, Bethlehem Ephratah, though thou be little among the thousands of Judah, yet out of thee shall he come forth unto me that is to be ruler in Israel: whose goings forth have been from old, from everlasting.

The prophets were messengers from God. They were preachers and teachers. While indicting the Israelites of breaking their covenant with God the prophets spoke messages from God of repentance, obedience, judgment, and salvation.

God vividly showed the Israelites his unconditional love for them by telling the prophet of doom, Hosea, to take himself a "wife of harlotry and children of harlotry, for the land has committed great harlotry by departing from the Lord." God literally told Hosea to take a woman with the heart of a harlot to be his wife. Hosea took Gomer for his wife. His experience was allegorical to God's experience with Israel. Israel had departed from God and had gone after strange gods. One of the sons of Hosea and Gomer was named Lo-Ammi (literally, not-my-people), "For you are not my people and I will not be your God." The people of Israel had utterly left the teaching of God. "She decked herself with her earrings and jewelry, and went after her lovers; but me she forgot," says the Lord (Hos. 2:13).

They were not destroyed for lack of zeal, for lack of emotions, for lack of caring, but for lack of knowledge.

Reading into chapter 4 we are told that God's people were destroyed "for lack of knowledge." Notice immediately that they were not destroyed for lack of zeal, for lack of emotions, for lack of caring, but for lack of knowledge. "Because thou hast rejected knowledge, I will also reject thee, that thou shalt be no priest to me; seeing thou hast forgotten the law of thy God, I will also forget thy children." Law is instruction. Law is teaching. Law is doctrine. Obeying God's law is necessary for salvation. Being informed of God's law is what reforms and transforms the lives of people. Without knowledge, there is no hope.

Knowledge is the information we need from God to be his people. In Deuteronomy 6, Moses exhorts the Israelites to hear God. In essence, he says, "Listen and do" the commandments of God. He admonishes the people to reform their lives in keeping with the commandments of God. Moses instructs them to teach the commands of God diligently to their children and to transform their own lives into righteousness by observing the commandments of God.

In the Old Testament, the purpose of the preaching and teaching was to inform the people of God of his commands. The power of that preaching and teaching was the ability to reform lives of iniquity. The promise of obeying God's word was the transformation of the heart of a harlot into a beloved child of God.

Questions

1. According to the author, the purpose of preaching and teaching is threefold. What three things can the word of God do for us?
2. What has always been God's avenue for transforming lives?
3. Why has entertainment become so much a part of our worship?
4. Give some possible reasons why Noah's generation did not listen to the preaching of Noah. Discuss similarities with the present generation.
5. What tribute did God pay to Abraham in Genesis 18? Name someone about whom you could say the same thing.
6. What did Moses command the people to do in Deuteronomy 31? What would happen if they did not do it?
7. What did Charles Hodge imply when he said that "some of us have become so open minded that our brains have fallen out"? What were the results of the Israelites' open-mindedness?
8. Why is Hebrew 11 called the "Roll Call of the Faithful"? What did their faith make them do?

9. What eventually happened to God's message as it was relayed through the priests? Compare their apostasy with current trends in the church.
10. What does *prophetes* mean? Give some examples.
11. Explain the function of the prophets in the Old Testament. Why were they necessary?
12. How did God allegorically show the Israelites how they had broken his heart?
13. According to Hosea, why were God's people destroyed? How does this principle apply to God's people today?

Thus Saith the Lord
New Testament

Preaching

"You sure are brave," a precious older Christian sister told me after a recent ladies' Bible class. One would have thought that I had just taught some new, profound revelation. The truth is, I had simply stated and applied to our lives simple biblical teaching.

The class under discussion was a class period discussing modesty and controlling our tongues. However, what this kind Christian woman said could have applied to a host of biblical teaching and preaching which offends our culture. Perhaps one has to be brave to stand up for the truth. Teaching the truth will cost you something. We know that many of the faithful in the Old Testament lost much because they chose to follow the teaching of God. We see numerous New Testament Christians who lost much, including their lives, in choosing to follow Jesus. Why do we think that being a Christian today and standing up for the truth will come cheaply?

Wilburn N. Smith, in his compelling 1945 work, *Therefore Stand*, speaks to this truth. He begins by noting that the apostle Paul urged all faithful Christians to "stand fast in the faith, quit you like [*act like*] men and be strong" (1 Cor. 16:13). He continues:

> The faith is, of course, as everyone recognizes, that body of truth which is elsewhere called the gospel, embracing belief in God, in Christ the Son of God, in Christ's death for sin, and his resurrection for our justification, in our own resurrection at the last day, eternal life in glory, and fellowship with the triune God . . . What those must do who have been saved by this gospel, and have put their trust in Christ as Saviour, no matter what costs, is to stand fast in the faith, i.e., we must never retreat from those great truths, without which there can be no saving gospel. It is not that in such a time of attack we are to stand fast in the theories of democracy, or

> to stand fast for some indefinite concept of "religion"; but that we are to stand fast in the faith, the faith set forth in the New Testament, and are not to allow men to push us back across that line of conviction that embraces a supernatural Christ, into the area of indifference or denial. We are to stand for the Church, in its great creeds, which are bulwarks for us carved out of the rocks of divine revelation. If we leave these fortresses, we will find ourselves helplessly exposed to every device of the enemies of God, and will be driven, step by step, and frequently league by league, back into the territory of agnosticism, if not absolute atheism, as many have experienced to their own sorrow.

The question concerning New Testament preaching and teaching today is whether or not we have left the fortresses of the bulwarks of faith and retreated from the great truths of the Bible or have we just become too weak or skeptical to preach and teach only the stark truth of the gospel?

The teaching and preaching of the New Testament, for which we are to stand regardless of the cost, has the purpose of informing us, the power of reforming us, and the promise of transforming us into the likeness of Christ. Paul tells the Corinthians,

> Know ye not that the unrighteous shall not inherit the kingdom of God? Be not deceived: neither fornicators, nor idolaters, nor adulterers, nor effeminate, nor abusers of themselves with mankind, nor thieves, nor covetous, nor drunkards, nor revilers, nor extortioners, shall inherit the kingdom of God. And such were some of you: but ye are washed but ye are sanctified, but ye are justified in the name of the Lord Jesus, and by the Spirit of our God (1 Cor. 6: 9-11).

The ultimate goal of biblical preaching and teaching is to bring the thinking of men and women into harmony with the thinking of Christ.

Several years ago I was teaching Bible to the young ladies in a Christian high school. During one of the classes on "Women's Role in the Church," I could see one young lady getting very uncomfortable and defensive. The next day I received a lengthy note from her telling me that she had talked to her preacher about our class and he told her that the Bible was just a love story from God to us and that it was not a book of rules by which we should live.

A novel cannot get us to Heaven.

If, indeed, the Bible is just a love story and not a book of doctrines by which we might mirror Christ and eventually be saved for eternity, then all of our preaching and teaching is vain. As a matter of fact, it is moot. A novel cannot get us to Heaven.

The truth of the matter is that the saving message of the gospel is so important and so necessary for our salvation that God came into the world as Christ to teach us himself. He may have come to fulfill the "love story" but he also came to teach us the conditions for salvation. Paul told the Galatians,

> Though we or an angel from heaven preach any other gospel unto you that that which we have preached unto you, let him be accursed. As we said before, so I say now again; If any man preach any other gospel unto you than that which ye have received, let him be accursed (Gal. 1: 8-9).

Jesus came to teach us about faith. He came to teach us so that we could teach others. Too many people think faith is simply belief. James tells us that "the devils believe and tremble (Jas. 2:19). Is that righteous faith? We know that Legion confessed Christ as the Son of God in Luke 8:28. Was that righteous faith? Is there anything in these two biblical examples that indicate belief only is what Christ came into the world to teach? The teaching of the New Testament calls the Christian not only to belief but to action on that belief which, in turn, produces righteous faith. Faith is following the teaching of Christ. There is no other physical manifestation of one's faith. There is no other way for the world to know that you are a follower of Christ.

If we confess one thing and live another then we are useless to our Lord.

One of the lessons we can glean from Ananias and Sapphira is that our actions must match our verbal affirmations. If we confess one thing and live another then we are useless to our Lord. We need desperately to be teaching and preaching this.

Jesus tells us in John 14:15, "If ye love me, keep my commandments." He goes on to say in verse 21, "He that hath my commandments, and keepeth them, he it is that loveth me: and he that loveth me shall be loved of my Father, and I will love him and will manifest myself to him." Continuing in John 15:10 Christ says, "If ye keep my commandments, ye shall abide in my love." How do we abide in the love of Christ? By keeping his commandments! There is no other way. We may *say* that we abide in his love, just like Ananias and Sapphira *said* they sold the field for a certain amount, but if we are not keeping his commandments we are not abiding in his love and our fate will be the same as theirs.

John becomes even more explicit in 1 John 2:3-4, when he tells us, "And hereby we do know that we know him, if we keep his commandments. He that saith I know him, and keepeth not his commandments, is a liar and the truth is not in him."

In our society, which is inundated with entertainment, we often confuse our preachers and Bible class teachers with actors and actresses, or with our favorite comedian or television news commentator. Our children's classes are filled with puppets, plays, and role playing because we have to compete with the entertainment of Barney or Blue's Clues and because our children's attention span only lasts for thirty-second sound bites! Unfortunately, many of the adults don't have much more of an attention span.

If you look at our college campuses—yes, even our Christian colleges—you will find that the sporting events are much better attended than the debates. The basketball game will be held in a wonderful new gymnasium with the capacity to hold hundreds or thousands, and the debates will be held in a small room in an obscure building. This shift from intellectual exercise to entertainment has caused a dumbing down of our society and, much to our misfortune, our preaching and teaching in the church have mirrored this change. We have an extremely hard time coming to contriteness and conviction while being entertained.

We have an extremely hard time coming to contriteness and conviction while being entertained.

We saw a dawning in the Old Testament that obedience was better than sacrifice and we see the same biblical truth in the New Testament. Paul tells us that "circumcision is nothing and uncircumcision is nothing, but the keeping of the commandments of God" (1 Cor. 7:19).

The question is not whether we have teachers who are brave enough to teach the truth, but rather are our teachers and preachers abiding in Christ? Do we love him? Are we obedient? If we are all of these things, we will discipline ourselves to study and to teach the truth whatever the cost.

Christ reminds us in the *Sermon on the Mount:* "Blessed are the pure in heart, for they shall see God" (Matt. 5:8). The pure in heart are those people who come to the Lord and to his word with no hidden agenda. It is very hard to view the scriptures through a "Liberation Theology" or a "Feminist Theology" or some other theology and come to the true meaning of New Testament teaching and preaching. Many times it is not the impotency of the message which fails to transform lives, but the hardness, the unbelief, or the preconceived ideas of the hearers which make it virtually impossible to see the will of God clearly. One must come to God and to his instruction with a pure heart—a heart that is listening and ready to obey God's will.

There is an urgent need for the church and for our preachers and teachers to return to the word of God. In a culture in which the battle is increasing in fervor against anything which resembles the word of God, or right or wrong, the only thing which has enough strength, vigor, timelessness, and power to sustain Christians, as well as the life of the body of Christ, is the word of God. It is the only message with the power to win souls.

Another aspect of our Christian universities which has weakened the Lord's church is that they are failing to turn out men who are learned in the scriptures and able to defend the truth. One of our children who went to a Christian university questioned everything scriptural he had ever been taught because he had professors (with doctorate degrees from various and sundry schools of theology) who were teaching predestination; questioning the biblical teaching of marriage, divorce, and remarriage; and challenging many other biblical truths. My husband and I studied with him for hours at a time, combating what was being taught at the Christian university. Thankfully, the truth of God's word prevailed and he is a gospel preacher. But how many other young minds have been corrupted?

Most young people who were brought up in Christian homes do not even understand why there is no piano in the church building.

Apologetics is a long lost art and most young people who were brought up in Christian homes do not even understand why there is no piano in the church building. Most of them consider the building the church. I have had young ladies say to me, "Oh! I shouldn't be wearing these shorts in the church." (Most of the time they were shorts that should not have been worn in public at all!) The underlying problem is a condemnation of our own generation. We have failed to preach and teach the word of God. We have not followed Moses' instruction in Deuteronomy 6 and taught our children "when thou sittest in thy house, and when thou walkest by the way, and when thou liest down, and when thou risest up (Deut. 6:7). Consequently, many have "forgotten the Lord" (Jer. 3:21) and as a result many will be lost.

We have been afraid of being called intolerant, unloving, or legalistic. But if there is only one gospel, which we profess to believe, then we should be teaching and preaching it. John says that there is salvation in no other: "He that hath the Son hath the life; he that hath not the Son of God hath not the life" (1 John 5:12). How do we know that we have the Son? By keeping his commandments! How do we learn the commandments? By being taught the word of God. We are not going to be saved by the teaching of *The Andy Griffith Show* or *Touched By an Angel*. We are not going to be saved by wonderful stories of our home life. We are not going to be saved by a twenty-minute sermon that leaves us feeling all warm and fuzzy inside. We are only going to be saved by preaching and teaching the gospel of Christ!

***We are not going to be saved by the teaching of* The Andy Griffith Show *or* Touched By an Angel.**

If your child came home from school with a math paper on which 3+3=9 was marked correctly, you might overlook it the first time. The second time, you would begin to question it and by the third time you would probably be meeting with the math teacher. She may say to you, "I know that 3+3=6 but I *feel like* 3+3=9 is close enough. In my class that will be all right." Would you be getting your child out of that math class? I think so!

If you went to the dentist with a toothache and he said that he needed to extract the tooth, you might agree. But if he said, "Go over to the hospital and get prepped for surgery because I *feel like* and *truly believe from the bottom of my heart* that the best way to get to the tooth would be to go up through your leg and then your abdomen and then your head and get to the tooth. Would you be heading over to the hospital? I think not! Why? Because medicine and math are both based on sound principles and not feelings. It appears to us that religion is the only area of our lives in which we are willing to base our eternal destination on our feelings rather than the teaching and commandments of Christ.

Many in the Lord's church are no longer teaching the word of God; rather they are appealing to the feelings and opinions of men. Facilitators have replaced teachers in Bible classes. The new method is designed to make each participant believe that his comments are valid, worthwhile, and acceptable. Such is the role of facilitator: to be supportive, open to suggestions, non-judgmental, and accepting, so no conclusions are drawn and no single standard is used to define a proper course of action. The method has long been used in support groups to build self-confidence, encouraging participants to express themselves more freely and to come to their own conclusions.

We who have been entrusted with the word of God must make sure we are not caught up in the cultural teaching methods of our time in a frenzied attempt just to keep the attention of the class. We are in danger of creating a generation of scriptural nitwits who may be "tossed to and fro and carried about with every wind of doctrine" (Eph. 4:14) because of a "zeal . . . not according to knowledge" (Rom. 10:2).

The Bible clearly teaches that he gave "some prophets, some evangelists; and some pastors and teachers; for the work of ministry, for the edifying of the body of Christ" (Eph. 4:11-12). Obviously not everyone is a teacher. We are warned in James 3:1, "My brethren, let not many of you become teachers, knowing that we shall receive a stricter judgment." Paul told Timothy to commit the things he had been taught to "faithful men who will be able to teach others also" (2 Tim. 2:2).

Timothy was admonished to "study [be eager, make every effort, be diligent] to show thyself approved unto God, a workman that needeth not to be ashamed, rightly dividing the word of truth" (2 Tim. 2:15). Timothy was told to avoid foolish and unlearned questions, knowing that they gender strife, to be apt to teach and to instruct people that oppose themselves so that they might come to repentance to the acknowledging of the truth in order that they might recover themselves out of the snare of the devil (2 Tim. 2:23-26). This type of godly conversion and repentance can come only when one is *informed* of the word of God. Then the power of that word and a love for the Lord will *reform* one's life. Ultimately, with commitment and continued study, one matures and becomes *transformed* into the image of Christ.

An elder is admonished to be "apt to teach" (1 Tim. 3:2) and to "hold fast the faithful word as he has been taught, that he may be able by sound doctrine both to exhort and to convince the gainsayers" (Tit. 1:9). Likewise, older women are instructed in Titus 2:3-5 to teach the younger women many virtues of the Christian life.

His commands are not optional, open for suggestion, or decided upon by a vote.

The doctrines and teachings of Christ were written to inform us. They were written for our education. Throughout the Old and New Testaments we are instructed by God to teach his commandments. His commands are not optional, open for suggestion, or decided upon by a vote. No sound doctrine is open for private interpretation (2 Pet. 1:20). "There is a way that seemeth right to man, but the end thereof are the ways of death" (Prov. 16:25). We must not rely on our own understanding. We must not preach and teach the agenda of our own private interpretation. Each of us would like to come up with some new, astounding truth but there really is nothing new under the sun. God is above all and in all and his word is the only lasting truth!

Christianity is a taught religion. That was true in the Old Testament and that is true in the New Testament. An eldership is responsible for seeing that sound doctrine is being preached and taught and that the blind are not leading the blind (Matt. 15:14).

Every preacher and teacher needs to have studied to show himself approved and able to teach. That takes discipline. The best teacher or preacher may not be the person with the best personality. It may not be the best-looking person. The best teacher or preacher may not be the person who can make the class laugh or the congregation comfortable. The best preachers and teachers are the ones who have the discipline to study and who know the word of God.

This past Father's Day, I heard a young married man preach one of the best lessons on child-rearing that I have ever heard. He readily admitted that he was not a father and that he was not preaching from experience, but from the word of God. He said he didn't know much about parenting personally, but he commented that he had a strong Christian father and he knew what God said about parenting. As a matter of fact, he knew the Bible extremely well, being able to quote many verses from memory. The lesson was tremendous and I prayed that this young man would raise his children according to the word of God and that life's experiences would not make him a lukewarm preacher. We tend to lose our conviction, our zeal, and our effectiveness when life's experiences make it difficult to believe what God says is true. I have seen many preachers and teachers change their teaching on marriage, divorce, and remarriage when someone in their own family divorces. I have seen many preachers who have become reluctant to teach biblical principles of parenting and fatherhood because of their own wayward children.

Many preachers and teachers change their teaching on marriage, divorce, and remarriage when someone in their own family divorces.

God's word does not change or become altered because of our own personal life experiences. His precepts are eternal and just as relevant in the twenty-first century as they were in the first century.

Unless we believe that the Bible is the inspired and infallible word of God, we will not be effective preachers and teachers; we will tend to give authority to creeds, manuals, our own consciences, the belief of the majority, cultural views, and subjectivity. The Holy Spirit tells us to "preach the word; be instant in season, out of season; reprove, rebuke exhort with all longsuffering and doctrine" (2 Tim. 4:2).

Teaching the truth of God cannot be a popularity contest. It never has been. It never will be. Remember, ultimately, only one vote counts.

Questions

1. Name some people in the Bible who lost much because of their desire to follow the Lord. Even though we may not lose our lives physically, what can we lose by choosing to follow and to teach the word of God?
2. Have we retreated from teaching the great truths of the Bible? Why or why not?
3. The teaching in the New Testament has a threefold purpose according to the author. What three things happen when the truth of the Bible is taught?
4. Is the Bible a love story from God? Is it more than that?
5. What is the physical manifestation of one's faith?
6. In 1 John 2:3-4 we are told how we know that we love him. How do we know?
7. What has been the effect of entertainment on the Lord's church and on Christians in general?
8. Explain what it means to be pure in heart.
9. Explain the difference between a facilitator and a teacher.
10. What is the elders' responsibility to the congregation in the area of biblical teaching?
11. Why do our life's experiences make us reluctant to teach biblical principles to others?
12. Do our personal life's experiences actually change the teaching of the Bible? Share scriptures with the class to support your answer.

Tithes and Offerings

Gloria Ingram

A quiet and stable leader, Gloria Ingram teaches with wisdom and grace to children, teens, and ladies. Her work in the church alongside Van, her husband of fifty-seven years, has extended over four southeastern states and abroad. For more than twenty-five years they have devoted much of their time to family service. Van was executive director of AGAPE of North Alabama for fourteen years. Gloria and Van have had as many as 168 children under their supervision at one time, placing many in adoptive homes. They have conducted home and family workshops, and also assisted local church outreach by providing family counseling to communities.

Gloria has served as an elder's wife in four congregations. Since 1990, Gloria and Van have found joy in working with Sojourners, serving as directors and co-directors for eight years. Mission work is no stranger to Gloria; she labored with Van in a recent endeavor on the west central coast of Florida in a planned community of 65,000.

All of these experiences have enhanced Gloria's effectiveness as an instructor. Ladies in Alabama, Florida, Mississippi, Tennessee, Indiana, and Scotland have been spiritually nourished by her teaching in classes, ladies' days, and workshops.

Gloria is the mother of a son, two daughters, and a foster daughter. She is grandmother, "Mama Glo," to fourteen grandchildren and five great-grandchildren. A native of Alabama—born in Tuscaloosa and reared in Ozark—it is appropriate that she and Van currently live in Vernon, Alabama.

Tithes and Offerings
Old Testament

Percentage Giving

The Awesomeness of God

Christians know that all things belong to God. "Indeed heaven and the highest heavens belong to the Lord, your God, also the earth with all that is in it (Deut. 10:14). He created us as living souls in his own image, surrounding us with the beauties of nature and blessings for our every need. "Behold, all souls are mine" (Ezek. 18:4). "And you shall remember the Lord your God, for it is he who gives you power to get wealth, that he may establish his covenant which he swore to your fathers, as it is this day" (Deut. 8:18).

Our Father's example of giving is exemplary. It is climaxed in the ultimate gift of his only begotten Son. By total commitment to his will he has promised blessings. At a time when our nation is in need of healing, note the words in 2 Chronicles 7:14:

> If my people are called by my name, shall humble themselves and pray and seek my face, and turn from their wicked ways; then I will hear from heaven, and will forgive their sin, and heal their land.

The Bible further says, "The eternal God is thy refuge and underneath are the everlasting arms" (Deut. 33:27).

To heal our land and feel the strength of his everlasting arms we must take action. Let us begin by diligently studying the Bible. May we purpose within our hearts to study with a desire to obey, becoming humble, holy, obedient, thankful servants of a loving, powerful Father. What an exciting challenge we face in the above truths to be faithful stewards of all that is entrusted to our care. The examples in the Old Testament are "written for our learning" and admonition (Rom. 15:4; 1 Cor. 10:11).

The Patriarchal Age

Cain and Abel

After God created Adam and Eve, he placed them in the garden with two simple instructions: (1) "multiply and replenish the earth" (Gen. 1:28) and (2) "tend the garden and keep it" (Gen. 2:15). There was one restriction: "Of the tree of the knowledge of good and evil, you shall not eat" (Gen. 2:17). The first account of a sacrifice being made is recorded in Genesis 4:4-5: "And the Lord respected Abel and his offering, but he did not respect Cain and his offering (Gen. 4:4-5). The reason for God's action was that by faith Abel offered to God a more excellent sacrifice than Cain, through which he obtained witness that he was righteous, God testifying of his gifts; and through it he being dead yet speaks" (Heb. 11:4).

We cannot allow Satan to control us or our possessions, for we belong to God.

Webster defines *righteous* as "acting in accord with divine or moral law; free from guilt or sin." Abel's good life speaks even after death. Because of his righteousness, Abel is a worthy example to us today. We cannot allow Satan to control us or our possessions, for we belong to God.

God later told Cain: "If you do well, will you not be accepted? And if you do not well, sin lies at the door. And its desire is for you, but you should rule over it" (Gen. 4:7). Because of Cain's unfaithfulness, we are admonished in the first verse of Jude: "Woe unto them! for they have gone in the way of Cain." Satan would like nothing more than to gain control over our lives, our thoughts, our money, and our time. Are we going to allow it?

The eighty-six year old father of a friend of ours and his grandson were baptized into Christ at the same time. The older man's son asked him what had moved him to obey God's will. Was it the grandson's example or something the preacher had said? His reply: "The godly example of my dear wife who has been dead for eighteen years." The power of a righteous life can teach even in death if we follow Abel's example.

Noah

Our hearts ache when we think of the evil surrounding us. Satan is truly at work in our individual lives, our homes, the church, our schools, the workplace, and our government. He is capturing our lives and busily trying to gain the lives of our children. Noah lived in a similar time.

> The Lord saw that the wickedness of man was great in the earth and that every intent of the thoughts of his heart was only evil continually. And the Lord was sorry that he had made man on the earth, and he was grieved in his heart (Gen. 6:5-6).

The Lord continues,

> I will destroy man whom I have created from the face of the earth, both man and beast, creeping thing and birds of the air, for I am sorry that I have made them. But Noah found grace in the eyes of the Lord . . . Noah was a just man, perfect in his generations. Noah walked with God . . . The earth also was corrupt before God, and the earth was filled with violence. So God looked upon the earth, and indeed it was corrupt; for all flesh had corrupted their way on the earth. And God said to Noah, The end of all flesh has come before Me, for the earth is filled with violence through them; and behold, I will destroy them with the earth (Gen. 6:7-13).

"Then Noah built an altar to the Lord . . . and offered burnt offerings on the altar."

Because of Noah's righteous life, God told him what to do to save himself and his family along with animals for reproduction and sacrifice. He gave specific instructions (Gen. 6, 7). "Thus Noah did; according to all that God commanded him, so he did" (Gen. 6:22). "And Noah did according to all that the Lord commanded him" (Gen. 7:5).

When the earth was dried, Noah, his family, and all the animals, went out of the ark.

> Then Noah built an altar to the Lord, and took of every clean animal, and of every clean bird, and offered burnt offerings on the altar. The Lord smelled the soothing aroma and promised never again to destroy every living thing as he had done. While the earth remains, seed time and harvest, cold and heat, winter and summer, and day and night shall not cease (Gen. 8:21-22).

And then a further promise: "I set my rainbow in the cloud, and it shall be for a sign of the covenant between me and the earth" (Gen. 9:13). May we never fail to value a righteous life in a world filled with evil.

Abraham

Abraham is the first one recorded as having given a tenth to a priest. In Genesis 14:18-20, after Melchizedek blessed him, Abraham gave him a tithe of all that he had (Heb. 7:1-2).

Earlier, when God told Abraham to leave his homeland and family, he obeyed. We find him building altars along the way and calling on the name of the Lord. When a famine arose, he went down to Egypt. It was as they were entering Egypt that he told Sarai to tell the Egyptians that she was his sister. We find no account of his building an altar while there. Does this not say something to us? We always need to be in the place where we can take God with us.

We always need to be in the place where we can take God with us.

The greatest sacrifice God asked of Abraham was his only son Isaac as a burnt offering. How difficult this must have been for him. Yet, we see him arising early with Isaac. He laid the wood on Isaac's back and carried the fire and a knife. He was prepared to complete the offering when the angel of the Lord stopped him. He feared God and was willing to offer his only son (Gen. 22:1-14).

In Genesis 22:16-18:

> By myself I have sworn, says the Lord, because you have done this thing, and have not withheld your son, your only son—blessing I will bless you, and multiplying I will multiply your descendants as the stars of the heaven and as the sand which is on the seashore; and your descendants shall possess the gate of their enemies. In your seed all the nations of the earth shall be blessed, because you have obeyed my voice.

Abraham made mistakes but he kept walking closer with God. "And the Scripture was fulfilled which says, Abraham believed God, and it was accounted to him for righteousness. and he was called the friend of God" (Jas. 2:23). Abraham obeyed God, leaving his homeland and offering his only son without questioning and complaining. This is a sobering thought for us who are blessed so abundantly, and asked to give so little by comparison. Too often, we are reluctant to leave our comfort zone on the church pew to share our fellowship with the visitor in our midst, to cheer the lonely, to encourage the weak, or to share the gospel with the lost.

Jacob

Jacob, the father of Israel, made a vow to God in Genesis 28:20-22. If God would be with him and allow him to return to the house of his fathers, he would give God a tenth of all that he received from God's hand. Jacob fled his father's house because of Esau. At the end of the day, he made a stone his pillow and lay down to sleep. In a dream God promised Jacob that he would be with him and bring him back to the land he had left. Upon awakening, Jacob set up the stone he had used as a pillow and poured oil on it. He then made a vow saying: "This stone which I have set as a pillow shall be God's house, and of all you give me I will surely give a tenth to you" (Gen. 28:22). Years later he returned and "built an altar there, and called the place El Bethel, because there God appeared to him as he was fleeing from his brother" (Gen. 35:6-7).

> ***"Of all you give me I will surely give a tenth to you"***

Mosaical Dispensation

The priests, of the tribe of Levi, were to offer the sacrifices for the people. Those sacrifices were to be of firstfruits, without spot or blemish. The presentation had to be according to a given plan, at the appointed place, and in God's prescribed way. Deuteronomy 12:32 states: "Whatever I command you, be careful to observe it; you shall not add to it nor take away from it." The books of the law frequently point out: "I am the Lord, do as I command, and heed the commandments."

God has always loved man; he asks of man only that which is for man's good. Satan's challenge has always been to bring us the heartache which results when man disobeys God.

Tithes

The Priestly Tithe

> Then the Lord said to Aaron, You have no inheritance in this land, nor shall you have any portion among them; I am your portion and your inheritance among them. Behold, I have given the children of Levi all the tithes in Israel as an inheritance in return for the work which they perform, the work of the tabernacle of meeting (Num. 18:20-21).

It was through the tithe that God provided a way for the priests to be supported by the hands of his people as the priests served the people in their offerings before God. The Levites in turn were to give a heave offering of the tithe they had received.

The Festival Tithe

The festival tithe was a gift of wine and oil, and the firstborn of the flocks and herds. It was to be offered and eaten before the Lord in the place where he chose to make his name abide. If the journey to that place was so far as to be difficult for the giver to carry the tithe, it could be sold and the money used to purchase the necessary items at the place God had chosen (Deut. 14:22-24). Verses 26 and 27 state:

> And you shall spend that money for whatever your heart desires: for oxen or sheep, for wine or similar drink, for whatever your heart desires; you shall eat there before the Lord your God, and you shall rejoice, you and your household. You shall not forsake the Levite who is within your gates, for he has no part nor inheritance with you.

How the Lord loved them! From the early days he planned for the happiness and the welfare of his people, if in return they would love and obey him. He is truly an awesome God.

The Charity Tithe

> At the end of every third year you shall bring out the tithe of that year and store it within your gates. And the Levite, because he has no portion nor inheritance with you, and the stranger and fatherless and widow who are within your gates, may come and eat and be satisfied, that the Lord your God may bless you in all the work of your hand which ye do (Deut. 14:28-29).

It was, and is, God's desire that his people be unselfish and aware of the needs of those about them. Our giving unselfishly will meet those needs and cause us to enjoy the blessing of helping others.

Other Offerings

Numerous other offerings were required besides the tithes. When God's people reaped the harvest, they were not to reap wholly the corners of their field (Lev. 19:9). They were not to go over a field a second time, nor could they go back to retrieve any sheaves they overlooked, nor to pick up any they dropped. They were also to leave some of the fruit of the grape vine and the olive tree for the fatherless, widow, and stranger. God wanted them to remember how it had been for their forefathers while they were slaves in Egypt. By their obedience, God would bless them in all the work of their hands. (Deut. 24:19-22).

Ruth tenderly cared for her mother-in-law Naomi by working in the fields. Boaz, the landowner, commanded his servants to drop bundles more frequently and not to rebuke Ruth when she gathered them.

As they were blessed, not by the might of their own hands but with God beside them, may we also be blessed with hearts ever tender toward those in need. With a willing, cheerful spirit, let us seek opportunities to relieve the suffering of those around us.

The people of God were to be diligent and punctual in making their offerings.

The people of God were to be diligent and punctual in making their offerings—not to delay in offering their best to the Lord (Exod. 22:29). Freewill offerings, as the Lord had blessed them, were to be given on other occasions, such as the Feast of Tabernacles (Deut. 16; Lev. 23).

All of the offerings were to be seasoned with salt (Lev. 2:13). Adam Clark said:

> Salt, was the opposite of leaven, for it preserved from putrification and corruption, and signified the purity and preserving fidelity that were necessary in the worship of God. Everything was seasoned with it, to signify the purity and perfection that should be extended through every part of the divine service, and through the hearts and lives of God's worshippers (Adam Clark's Commentary, vol. 1, p. 515).

Building the Tabernacle

Moses gathered all of the people together to tell them of God's command to build the tabernacle as a place where he could abide in their midst and meet with them. The people were to bring offerings of gold, silver, and bronze; blue, purple, and scarlet thread; and fine linen, goat's hair, oil, spices, and acacia wood (Exod. 35:5-9). Four times in Exodus 35 they were reminded that their gifts must be from willing hearts. Then all of the gifted artisans, in whose hearts God had put wisdom and understanding, did the work (Exod. 36:1).

The people brought more than enough (Exod. 36:6-7). "And the people were restrained from bringing; for the material they had was sufficient for all the work to be done . . . indeed too much." The people had seen the need. Their spirits had been stirred within them, and they were willing to give—even to the point of having to be stopped from bringing offerings to the Lord.

May our hearts be stirred as we see the souls needing to be taught and so many in need of our care and benevolence. May we, from willing hearts, arise to the challenge. The choice is ours.

David

As a result of David's rebellion in taking a census of the children of Israel, God began punishing the people and many died. David was distressed. He admitted his sin and asked God to let his hand be against him and his father's house, and not against the people (2 Sam. 24:17). God directed David to go up to the threshing floor of Araunah, the Jebusite and erect an altar there. When Araunah saw David and his servants coming, he bowed before the king and inquired about their mission. Upon being informed, Araunah tried to give the threshing floor, oxen for burnt sacrifice, implements needed in making the sacrifices, and the yokes of oxen for wood. Refusing the offer David said: "No, but I will surely buy it from you for a price, nor will I offer burnt offerings to the Lord my God with that which costs me nothing." With this statement of purpose, David bought the threshing floor, and offered burnt offerings and peace offering, and God withdrew the plague from against the people of Israel (2 Sam. 24:20-25).

Adam Clark, in commenting on the principle expressed by David in verse 24, says:

> It is a maxim from heaven: "Honor the Lord with thy substance." He who has a religion that costs nothing, has a religion that is worth nothing: nor will any man esteem the ordinances of God, if those ordinances cost him nothing. Had Araunah's noble offer been accepted, it would have been Araunah's sacrifice, not David's; nor would it have answered the end of turning away the displeasure of the Most High. It was David who sinned, not Araunah; therefore David must offer sacrifice, and at his own expense too (Adam Clark, vol. 2, p. 380).

The intent expressed by David is a great example to apply to giving of our time, as well as our money and other material things. Many pews are filled but few sacrifices are made. We need to examine ourselves and be committed as living sacrifices which is our reasonable service (Rom. 12:1-2). We too need to be ready to confess our sins and change our actions as David did.

The Generosity of Solomon

Solomon had been commissioned to build the temple. Having faithfully finished the task, he dedicated it with a prayer unto God. Following his prayer, the Bible states:

> Then the king and all the people offered sacrifices before the Lord. King Solomon offered a sacrifice of twenty-two thousand bulls and one hundred and twenty sheep. So the king and all the people dedicated the house of God (2 Chron. 7:4-5).

God's answer to Solomon is soul stirring. "Then the Lord appeared to Solomon by night and said to him, I have heard your prayer and have chosen this place for myself as a house of sacrifice" (7:12). The beauty of the temple and the offerings rendered there became symbolic of the beauty of the church of the New Testament and of the lives of believers (1 Cor. 3:17; 6: 19). Our Lord loves us and he will bless us, if we fully dedicate ourselves to him.

The Widow of Zarephath

As Elijah approached the city of Zarephath, he saw the woman picking up sticks near the gate of the city (1 Kings 17:8-24). He asked her for a little water and a morsel of bread. She replied that there was only enough meal and oil to make bread for her and her son. They would eat it and die. Elijah responded to her:

> Do not fear; go and do as I have said, but make me a small cake from it first and bring it to me; and afterward make some for yourself and your son. For thus says the Lord God of Israel: The bin of flour will not be used up, nor shall the jar of oil run dry, until the day the Lord sends rain on the earth (1 Kings 17:13-14).

She was afraid she might be tempted to spend God's part.

She did not fear and did as Elijah directed. Her measure of faith is manifested by her wonderful example of generosity.

A Christian woman, a teacher of children's Bible classes for many years, married a soldier during World War I and had two children. After the war he told her he was going back to the family she did not know he had. She never saw him again. During the Great Depression of the 1930s, she worked long and hard to meet the basic needs of her family, but her first commitment was to God. On Friday, when she received her meager salary in cash, she immediately separated the cleanest of the bills to give back to God the next Sunday. She dared not go to the grocery store on the way home for fear she might be tempted to spend God's part. She, like the widow of Zarapheth, has left us a great example.

The Notable Woman of Shunam

> Now it happened one day, that Elisha went to Shunam, where there was a notable woman and she persuaded him to eat food. So it was as often as he passed by, he would turn in there to eat food (2 Kings 4:8).

Knowing Elisha was a man of God, the woman made a request of her husband: "Please, let us make a small room on the wall, and let us put a bed for him there, and a table and a lamp stand, so it will be, whenever he comes he can turn in there" (2 Kings 4:10). The husband agreed and they built a simple, comfortable place for Elisha.

She was hospitable, receptive, and thoughtful in planning for the prophet. She showed no thought of what she might get in return, but because of her willingness to give, God blessed her with a son.

The Young Israelite Slave Girl

Naaman was a great and noble commander, the Lord having given victory to Syria through him (2 Kings 5:1-2). Despite his greatness, he was a leper. A young slave girl, captured in Israel, and a servant to his wife, was concerned about her master. She said to her mistress: "If only my master were with the prophet in Samaria! For he would heal him of his leprosy" (2 Kings 5:3). Naaman heeded her words and went to the prophet's house. Elisha sent his servant out to tell Naaman to go and dip himself seven times in the river Jordan. Even though Naaman was reluctant to obey this simple command, his servant urged him to do so. Following his seventh dip, his flesh was restored like that of a little child (2 Kings 5:9-14).

She took the time to give of herself in sharing with her master and his wife the power of the God of Israel.

The courage and kindness of this young girl helped Naaman find healing. She took the time to give of herself in sharing with her master and his wife the power of the God of Israel. It is a fervent prayer that those of all ages who read this will be encouraged to follow her example. There is something each of us can share to bless the lives of others. Let us stir up our gifts and use them to his glory, helping to cleanse a leprous world.

Haggai Records the Lack of Concern of God's People

Our Lord loves us and he will bless us if we fully dedicate ourselves to him. Haggai was sent to encourage God's people to rebuild the temple. They came saying the time was not yet come that the Lord's temple should be rebuilt. Listen to the words of the Lord spoken by the prophet:

> Is it time for you yourselves to dwell in your paneled houses, and this temple to be in ruins? Now therefore, thus says the Lord of hosts: Consider your ways! you have sown much and bring in little; you eat, but do not have enough; you drink, but you are not filled with drink; you clothe yourselves, but no one is warm; and he who earns wages earns wages to put into a bag with holes. Thus says the Lord of hosts: Consider your ways! Go up the mountains and bring wood and build the temple that I may take pleasure in it and be glorified . . . you looked for much, and yet it came to little; and when you brought it home, I blew it away. Why? . . . because of my house that is in ruins, while every one of you runs to his own home. Therefore the heavens about you withhold the dew, and the earth withholds its fruit. For I called for a drought on the land and the mountains, on the grain and the new wine and the oil, on whatever the ground bring forth, on men and livestock, and on all the labor of your hands (Hag. 1:4-11).

The people "obeyed the voice of the Lord their God, and the words of Haggai the prophet, as the Lord had sent him; and the people feared the presence of the Lord." The Lord responded through Haggai: "I am with you, says the Lord" (Hag. 1:12-13).

The above, quoted in detail, should reinforce the power of God's word and his desires for obedience in our lives. Let us be motivated to fear God—have profound reverence for; to be awe-stricken by—and to obey his commands.

If God spoke to us directly today, would he deliver a similar message? Are we absorbed with building fine houses while the world is without Christ? The Lord wants his people to know who is in control and from whom their blessings come. He wants the same concern for him and his work from us as he wanted from those of former times.

Malachi

Malachi is to be commended for his faithfulness and courage as he prophesied when the conditions in Israel were deplorable. How grieved the Lord must have been because of the wickedness and selfishness of the people. They were offering the blind, the lame, the sick, and the stolen animals as sacrifices (Mal. 1:8, 13). Because God demanded the choice of the flocks and herds, he refused to accept their offerings. He admonished the people to return to him, and he would return unto them (Mal. 3:7). Their response was: "In what way shall we return?" Though their defiled sacrifices had profaned the altar, they seemed to be oblivious to any offense committed against God. The priests not only participated in the inferior sacrifices, they were charged with robbing God. They asked: "In what way have we robbed you?" God's answer? "In tithes and offerings." God cursed them because "you have robbed me, even this whole nation." Then he urged them, "Bring all of your tithes into the storehouse, and try me now in this, says the Lord of hosts, if I will pour out for you such blessing that there will not be room enough to receive it." (Mal. 3:8-10.)

Though their defiled sacrifices had profaned the altar, they seemed to be oblivious to any offense committed against God.

Even though their sin was great, their loving God was desirous of their repentance. The choice was theirs to obey or to refuse. Malachi 3:16 tells of those who changed; fearing God, encouraging one another, and meditating on his name.

Malachi indirectly pleads with each of us to search our hearts carefully and prayerfully to see if we are offering our second-best to God, robbing him by using our blessings selfishly on ourselves. God wants our pure offerings.

Closing Thoughts

May we steadfastly plant in our hearts God's commands to the Israelites in regard to their giving:

1. Firstfruits without spot or blemish—the best.
2. According to God's plan.
3. At the place he chose.
4. At the time he chose.
5. Worshipers holy—priests and the providers of the sacrifices.
6. A tenth as required, as well as freewill offerings.
7. Cheerfully giving from a willing heart.
8. On time—never delinquent or tardy.
9. Gifts seasoned with salt.

Remember, God wants his children to realize he is our creator and owns everything—even our souls. He has given us the choice of obeying or not obeying his will. He has promised to keep us under his everlasting arms if we are faithful to him. The Israelites have given us great examples of both choices. Obey the will of God and be blessed, or disobey and be cursed.

Questions

1. To whom do all things belong, even our souls?
2. What did God tell the Israelites they must do in order to obtain forgiveness and heal their land?
3. Why was Abel's sacrifice accepted and Cain's rejected?
4. Why were Noah and his family not destroyed in the flood?
5. What was the greatest burnt offering Abraham was asked to make to God?
6. What did Jacob vow to do, if God would allow him to return to his father's house?
7. What tribe was known as the priestly tribe of Israel?
8. Name the three tithes mentioned. Explain each.
9. Name some of the other offerings. With what they were to be seasoned?
10. With what attitude of heart does God wish us to give?
11. Describe the attitude of the Israelites as they gave materials for the tabernacle.
12. How did David react when Araunah wanted to give the place to build an altar for making sacrifices to God?

13. On what occasion did Solomon offer a sacrifice of 22,000 bulls and 120 sheep to the Lord?
14. Describe the faith of the widow of Zarapheth.
15. Contrast, or compare, the actions of the notable woman of Shunam with our use of our homes. How given are we to hospitality to God's servants, the weak, the lost, and even our families today?
16. Do we have the courage of the young Israelite slave girl, to bring those who need the cleansing from the leprosy of sin into contact with the cleansing power of the gospel?
17. When Haggai rebuked the children of God for not building the temple, what were they doing?
18. What are we busy doing today?
19. Name nine commands of God, concerning giving in the Old Testament.
20. Are we ready to study God's word and to offer him the first-fruits of our lives and our possessions?

Purpose Giving

In the previous chapter we noted the awesomeness of God:

- All things in heaven and earth belong to God.
- We belong to him—"all souls are mine."
- What we gain or accomplish is by his power, not ours.

These truths are reinforced in the New Testament. Paul asks:

> Or do you not know that your body is the temple of the Holy Spirit, which is in you, whom you have from God, and you are not your own? For you were bought at a price; therefore glorify God in your body, and in your spirit, which are God's (1 Cor. 6:19-20).

Christ "gave himself for us, that he might redeem us from every lawless deed and purify for himself his own special people, zealous for good works" (Titus 2:14). As stewards we must be committed to taking care of the God's possessions that he has entrusted to our care: "Moreover, it is required in stewards that one be found faithful" (1 Cor. 4:2). "As each one has received a gift, minister it to one another, as good stewards of the manifold grace of God" (1 Pet. 4:10). Each one of us shall have to give an account to God as to our stewardship (Rom. 4:12).

God's love is expressed in Romans 5:8: "But God demonstrates his own love toward us, in that while we were still sinners, Christ died for us." Again, in John 3:16: "For God so loved the world, that he gave his only begotten Son, that whoever believes in him should not perish but have everlasting life."

In the Old Testament, the imperfect and temporal priests had to offer sacrifices continually for themselves and for the people. In contrast "Jesus has become our surety of a better covenant" (Heb. 7:22). By his continuing forever, his is an unchangeable priesthood. In Hebrews 7:25-28, we see the great blessing we have in Christ Jesus, our High Priest.

> Therefore he is also able to save to the uttermost those who come to God through him, since he always lives to make intercession for them. For such a High Priest was fitting for us, who is holy, blameless, undefiled, separate from sinners, and has become higher than the heavens; who does not need daily, as those high priests, to offer up sacrifices, first for his own sins and then for the people's, for this he did once for all when he offered up himself. For the law appoints as high priests men who have weakness, but the word of the oath, which came after the law; appoints the Son who has been perfected forever.

Christians as priests may offer praise, give thanks, and make sacrifices to the Father through Christ, our High Priest: "For there is one God, and one mediator between God and men, the Man Christ Jesus" (1 Tim. 2:5). Note further,

> Therefore, in all things he had to be made like his brethren, that he might be a merciful and faithful High Priest in things pertaining to God, to make propitiation for the sins of the people. For in that he himself has suffered, being tempted, he is able to aid those who are tempted (Heb. 2:17-18).

Christ, along with his Father, is our ultimate example of giving.

> Let this mind be in you which was also in Christ Jesus, who, being in the form of God, did not consider it robbery to be equal with God, but made himself of no reputation, taking the form of a bondservant, and coming in the likeness of men. And being found in appearance as a man, he humbled himself and became obedient to the point of death, even the death of the cross (Phil. 2:5-8).

"Do not forget to do good and to share, for with such sacrifices God is well pleased."

As he prayed in Gethsemane he asked the Father three times, "If it is possible, let this cup pass from me—but not as I will but as you will" (Matt. 26:36-46). "Therefore . . . let us continually offer the sacrifice of praise to God, that is, the fruit of our lips, giving thanks to his name. But do not forget to do good and to share, for with such sacrifices God is well pleased" (Heb. 13:15-16).

With Christ as our High Priest, what is to be the pattern by which we offer our sacrifices, freewill offerings, and gifts? We, too, need to do all things according to the pattern. To know the pattern takes a personal, diligent study of the word, with hearts desiring to do his will, not ours.

Characteristics of the Pattern

> Now concerning the collection for the saints, as I have given orders to the churches of Galatia, so you must do also: On the first day of the week let each one of you lay something aside, storing up as he may prosper, that there be no collections when I come (1 Cor. 16:1-2).

Regular Giving

We are commanded to give on the first day of the week. The work of the local congregation is usually planned with the giving of the congregation in mind. Christian should consider that failure to follow this pattern, whether at home or away, can disrupt good works. Being away from the local congregation does not diminish the need for individual Christians to financially support the local work.

> ***The first day of the week is not the only time we can give of ourselves.***

The first day of the week is not the only time we can give of our physical possessions and of ourselves to the Lord. Just as the Israelites made their freewill offerings, after giving their tithes, we can "do good to all, especially those of the household of faith" (Gal. 6:10). Jesus went about doing good (Acts 10:38). We, too, should realize that the need of another is the opportunity of a Christian.

Individual Giving

"Let each one of you . . ." (1 Cor. 16:2). Many members of the church excuse themselves from giving by coasting on the efforts of others. It is good for all of the family members, even non-wage earners, to share in giving. One man took the position that since his wife did not earn the income, it was his privilege alone to decide what would be given to the Lord. This Christian wife, not willing to be deprived of her individual responsibility, raised and sold roses so she, too, could give to the Lord.

Christian parents need to begin early to teach their children this needed lesson. Each family member can participate regularly in giving back to God a portion of that which has been entrusted to him or her. Learning early to take part in this fellowship can be a meaningful lesson for children, but also a great example to others. It is especially important for children to practice putting aside God's part first, once they are old enough to get an allowance or to earn their own money.

The parents of one of our grandsons began early to train their children to give. They also felt that it was good to teach them to give more than a small coin. Consequently, from the time they were able to reach up and put in their own contribution, they gave folding money. When our grandson was five, an older friend was sitting with him during worship. As time approached for the basket to pass, he looked at his friend and asked if he had anything to give. The friend shook his head negatively. Our grandson immediately tore his bill in two and gave half of it to his friend. We have often wondered what the ones counting the contribution thought upon finding two halves of a bill in the plate.

Purposeful Giving

"Let each one of you lay something aside, storing up as he may prosper" (1 Cor. 16:2). To purpose is to plan what you will give back to God. We each know in our hearts how much we have been blessed by a loving Father. In reality, we and all we possess belong to him. The question is not "how little may we give" but "how much can we give." Remember, we are stewards of all God. Purpose the maximum, not the minimum!

Purpose the maximum, not the minimum!

Remember the example of the Christian widow, mentioned in the previous chapter, who was left with two children. Even on her meager salary, she purposed to lay aside not only the first part, but the cleanest part of her pay for the Lord. She fully recognized that what was entrusted to her care was not hers, but the Lord's. Unfortunately, some give leftovers. God has never accepted the dross or chaff of our blessings.

Christians are not commanded to tithe, nor are we commanded to give equally, but equitably. Each one of us should prayerfully purpose in our hearts, giving a rightful amount of our blessings back to God. By laying it aside in a safe place, we are less likely to be tempted to use it for something else. A casual observation, which we may try to avoid, indicates that many have made no special plan to give, but on the spur of the moment choose something from what they happen to have with them. Sometimes, not having the amount they are willing to give, they do not give at all.

In 1956 a young couple, with two small children, moved into the city and began worshiping where my husband was preaching. The young mother was a member of the church. It was obvious that they were heavily in debt. The young man obeyed the gospel and soon after his conversion, the preacher taught a lesson on the "Joy of Giving." That same week, this couple went out and borrowed the money to consolidate their debts for the sole purpose of being able to give to the Lord. To this day, they have joyfully made a practice of considering God first in all of their blessings. Their dedication, growth, and liberality through the years has been a wonderful example for all who know them.

God expects the firstfruits, the best, of what we have to offer. This of necessity would require diligence as good stewards. This principle is so aptly illustrated in the parable of the talents (Matt. 25:14-30). We each are to do according to our several abilities. The one-talent man was not condemned because he possessed less, but because he was afraid, wicked, and lazy. We are to redeem the time (Eph. 5:16). Eternity itself is at stake. "For God has not given us a spirit of fear, but of power and of love and of a sound mind" (2 Tim. 1:7). As faithful stewards, we have the power of God behind us.

Christians give back to God in direct proportion to our degree of commitment.

Liberal Giving

Paul tells us in 2 Corinthians 8:1-5,

> Moreover brethren, we make known to you the grace of God bestowed on the churches of Macedonia: that in great trial of affliction the abundance of their joy and their deep poverty abounded in the riches of their liberality. For I bear witness that according to their ability, yes, and beyond their ability, they were freely willing, imploring us with much urgency that we would receive the gift and fellowship of the ministering to the saints. And not only as we had hoped, but they first gave themselves to the Lord, and then to us by the will of God.

Several qualities contributed to the liberality of the Macedonians. They joyfully served and submitted themselves to the Lord. They were freely willing to give, even beyond their ability. Why? Because they first gave themselves to the Lord. Christians give back to God in direct proportion to our degree of commitment to Him and to the priority we give the church in our lives as we "seek first the kingdom of God and his righteousness" (Matt. 6:33).

Jesus, sitting opposite the treasury, saw many who were rich putting in much. Then one poor widow dropped in two mites—a fraction of a penny. Jesus called his disciples and related to them what he had seen, saying:

> Assuredly, I say to you that this poor widow has put in more than all those who have given to the treasury; for they have given out of their abundance, but she out of her poverty put in all that she had, her whole livelihood (Mark 12:41-44).

Both the Macedonians and the poor widow gave liberally out of their poverty. Paul told the Corinthians that the Macedonians had willingly given beyond their ability. He further exhorted the Corinthians: "But as you abound in everything—in faith, in speech, in knowledge, in all diligence, and in your love for us—see that you abound in this grace also" (2 Cor. 8:7). In 2 Corinthians 8:9, Paul further reminds Christians, "For you know the grace of our Lord Jesus Christ, that though he was rich, yet for your sakes he became poor, that you through his poverty might become rich."

In family relationships, when we give ourselves to each other without reservation, our love and willingness to give know no bounds. What better proof is there of our love than to give ourselves to the Lord? Paul admonished the Corinthian brethren: "Therefore show to them, and before the churches the proof of your love and of our boasting on your behalf" (2 (Cor. 8:24). He further teaches:

> So let each one give as he purposes in his heart, not grudgingly or of necessity; for God loves a cheerful giver. And God is able to make all grace abound toward you, that you; always having all sufficiency in all things, may have an abundance for every good work (2 Cor. 9:7-8).

Note these meaningful words as Paul continues,

> As it is written: He has dispersed abroad, he has given to the poor . . . his righteousness endures forever. Now may he who supplies seed to the sower, and bread for food, supply and multiply the seed you have sown and increase the fruits of your righteousness while you are enriched in everything for all liberality, which causes thanksgiving through us to God. For the administration of this service not only supplies the needs of the saints, but also is abounding through many thanksgivings to God, while through

> the proof of this ministry, they glorify God for the obedience of your confession to the gospel of Christ, and for your liberal sharing with them and all men, and by their prayer for you, who long for you because of the exceeding grace of God in you. Thanks be to God for his indescribable gift! (2 Cor. 9:9-15.)

Adam Clarke commenting on 2 Corinthians 9:13 remarks:

> By the experiment of this ministration in the preceding and following verses, the apostle enumerates the good effects that would be produced by their liberal almsgiving to the poor saints at Jerusalem, (1) The wants of the saints would be supplied, (2) many thanksgivings would thereby be rendered unto God, (3) the Corinthians would thereby give proof of their subjection to the gospel, and (4) the prayers of those relieved would ascend up to God in the behalf of their benefactors (vol. 4, p. 353).

We prove our love for the Father by our actions. All that we do is made possible by him, and all we do is to be done to his glory. "Being filled with the fruits of righteousness, which are by Jesus Christ, to the glory and praise of God" (Phil. 1:11). "For of him and through him and to him are all things, to whom be glory forever. Amen" (Rom. 11:36). We prove our love by our liberality.

We prove our love by our liberality.

Giving necessitates cheerful and thankful hearts, whether it be with our money, our time, or our talents. Paul offers thanks to God who

> always leads us in triumph in Christ, and through us diffuses the fragrance of his knowledge in every place. For we are to God the fragrance of Christ among those who are being saved and among those who are perishing (2 Cor. 2:14-15).

Thankful hearts recognize their dependence upon God. He desires our praise and thankfulness, ever giving the glory to his name in all we do.

Paul's instruction in 1 Corinthians 16:1-2 eliminates other methods of fundraising. God has spoken—we should cheerfully and faithfully obey each command.

God knows us so well. His plan prompts personal soul searching as we plan our giving. There is no favoritism or comparison on his part. His great love and sacrifice for us, in the giving of his only begotten Son, leads us to give sacrificially from a willing and cheerful heart, not grudgingly nor of necessity. When we have obeyed according to the pattern, there will be resources for an ample program of evangelism and benevolence.

"All things were done according to the pattern" is mentioned four times in regard to the building of the tabernacle. Our eternal happiness, and that of those we influence, depends upon submitting to our Father's will. We must purpose in our hearts to submit ourselves to the Father's will—as Jesus did—to exalt his name among men.

God's word is replete with examples, both negative and positive, of giving. As we consider a few, let us keep in mind God's ultimate sacrifice—his only begotten Son. Contrast this mind with that of Judas Iscariot, who betrayed him (Matt. 26:14-15). The name Jesus brings an overflow of emotions, among which are peace and joy. However, Judas reminds us of how the love of money destroys him.

Ananias and Sapphira, while putting on the appearance of virtue and liberality, were compelled by greed to hold back a part of the money from the sale of their property (Acts 5:1-11). Peter asked him some sobering questions:

> Ananias, why has Satan filled your heart to lie to the Holy Spirit and keep back part of the price of the land for yourself? While it remained, was it not your own? And after it was sold, was it not in your own control? Why have you conceived this thing in your heart? You have not lied to men but to God. When he had heard these words, he fell down and died.

We are familiar with the rest of this story. His wife came to the apostle about three hours later, not knowing what had happened to her husband. Peter found that deceit was also in her. She joined her husband in death. Others may never know the degree of our liberality. Christians should know that it is futile to try to hide from God (Gen. 3:8-10).

In Luke 12:15-21, Jesus warned of covetousness by telling the story of a certain rich man, whose land had yielded plentifully. Upon seeing his bounty, his thoughts turned inward, thinking what he could do. He used the personal pronoun *I* six times, and *my* five times as he made plans to take it easy—to eat, drink, and be merry. "But God said to him, Thou fool! This night your soul will be required of you. Then whose will these things be which you have provided?" (Luke 12:20.) David, in Psalms 39:6, lamented: "Surely every man walks about like a shadow; surely they busy

"Thou fool! This night your soul will be required of you."

themselves in vain; he heaps up riches, and does not know who will gather them."

We live in an "I" and "my" society? Do we seek the welfare of others or our own gratification? Several years ago, the late and beloved Mary Oler, in speaking to a ladies' group, raised the question: "Is the wife and mother working outside the home because she has to, or is it for a 'bigger loaf of bread'?"

"Is the mother working outside the home for a 'bigger loaf of bread'?"

God's people can make a difference by ridding themselves of selfishness and using their resources to show Christ to a lost world. Let us begin at home, encouraging each family member to perform at his or her best. There is no room in a Christian's heart for selfishness or covetousness. The rich man was consumed by both.

A rich young man, who had a divided heart, came running to Jesus and kneeling down before him asked what he should do to inherit eternal life. Jesus loved him and responded that he should keep the commandments. The young man answered that he had always done this, and asked, "What lack I yet?" Jesus, knowing his heart, told him to go and sell all that he had, give it to the poor, take up the cross and follow him, laying up treasure in heaven. "But he was sad at this word, and went away sorrowful for he had great possessions." Jesus told his disciples: "How hard it is for them who have riches to enter the kingdom of God" (Matt. 19:16-22; Mark 10:17-23).

Adam Clarke, commenting on this passage said:

> To be complete, to have thy business finished, and all hindrances to thy salvation removed, go and sell that thou hast—go and dispose of thy possessions, to which it is evident his heart was so much attached, and give to the poor—for thy goods will be a continual snare to thee if thou keep them: and thou shalt have treasures in heaven—the loss, if it can be called such, shall be made amply up to thee in that eternal life about which thou inquires; and come and follow me—be my disciple, and I will appoint thee to preach the Kingdom of God to others. This was the usual call which Christ gave to his disciples (Matt. 4:19; 8:22; 9:9; Mark 2:14). It is pretty evident that he intended to make him a preacher of salvation. How many, by their attachment to filthy lucre, have lost the honor of becoming or continuing ambassadors for the Most High! Men undergo great agony of mind while they are in suspense between love of the world and the love of their souls. When the first absolutely predominates, then they enjoy a factitious rest through a false peace: When the latter has the upper hand,

> then they possess true tranquility of mind, through the peace of God that passeth knowledge (vol. 5, p. 193).

The apostle Paul exhibits the opposite response of that of the rich young man. A devout Jew with much authority, he was from Tarsus of Cilicia and therefore a Roman citizen. Trained by Gamaliel according to the strictness of the Jewish laws, he was zealous toward God as he persecuted Christians. When Paul realized he was wrong in his belief, he left a position of power and prestige to become the persecuted (Acts 22). What a changed life we see as he totally committed himself to the Lord.

Paul told us of the peace that he felt in forsaking all for Christ. In Philippians 2:14-16, he urged disciples of Christ "to do all things without complaining and disputings—children of God without fault in the midst of a crooked and perverse generation, among whom you shine as lights in the world, holding fast the word of life." Paul gave positive directions which, when followed, will keep those who are rich in this world from having a divided heart.

> Command those who are rich in this present age not to be haughty, nor to trust in uncertain riches, but in the living God, who gives us richly all things to enjoy. Let them do good, that they be rich in good works, ready to give, willing to share, storing up for themselves a good foundation for the time to come, that they may lay hold on eternal life (1 Tim. 6:17-19).

We each have gifts we can use to his glory. Would these not be seen as "free-will offerings" given to help, encourage, strengthen, and to comfort others? In many instances our caring—giving of ourselves—leads others to desire to become children of God. Jesus "began both do and to teach" (Acts 1:1).

Dorcas used her gift of sewing to provide clothes for the many widows at Joppa (Acts 9:36-42). Aquila and Priscilla shared their home with Paul while he was teaching at Corinth (Acts 18:1-4). Lazarus, Mary, and Martha provided for Jesus the nearest thing he had to an earthly home (Luke 10:38-41). On a visit there, he spoke of "choosing the good part," a lesson so vitally needed today. If we truly believe the words of Jesus, "it is more blessed to give than to receive" (Acts 20:35), our entire life will be a stewardship for the Lord.

"It is more blessed to give than to receive"

I beseech you therefore, brethren, by the mercies of God, that you present your bodies a living sacrifice, holy, acceptable to God, which is your reasonable service. And do not be conformed to this world, but be transformed by the renewing of your mind, that you may prove what is that good and acceptable and perfect will of God (Rom. 12:1-2).

Is not our response in giving ourselves to God in proportion to his greatness, his goodness, his example of sacrifice? He desires and expects the firstfruits of our lives to be in total submission to his will. He is our Father—we are to please him, not ourselves. Doing this abundantly blesses the giver.

"And whatsoever you do, do it heartily, as to the Lord and not to men" (Col. 3:23). Webster defines *heartily* as "with all sincerity, wholeheartedly; with zest or gusto." Let us be stewards for God with the same zest and wholeheartedness we would have if striving for the Olympic gold medal. Our awesome God deserves the best from his stewards, and the reward will surpass that of a gold medal or any honor man could bestow upon us—eternal life. Paul encourages us: "I can do all things through Christ who strengthens me" (Phil. 4:13).

Is it not time that we as his body show by the way we use our blessings from God that we are in this world, but not of this world? (John 17:16.) "For where your treasure is, there your heart will be also" (Matt. 6:21). "Each of us shall give account of himself to God" (Rom. 14:12). We have the opportunity and joy to show love and respect for God by serving him with a heart that is not greedy, selfish, or divided, but one that is willing to make any sacrifice joyfully in his cause.

Our task is to offer our sacrifice of self in a way that will be palatable to all with whom we come in contact.

The word of God guides us perfectly as to how we should give—the choice is ours. God help us to awaken and to meet the challenge before us. In the Old Testament every sacrifice had to be offered with good salt. Jesus said, "You are the salt of the earth; but if the salt loses its flavor, how shall it be seasoned?" (Matt. 5:13.) Our task is to offer our sacrifice of self, well seasoned in God's word, in a way that will be palatable to all with whom we come in contact.

"He who finds his life will lose it, and he who loses his life for my sake will find it" (Matt. 10:39).

Questions

1. What is the responsibility of a steward?
2. We are stewards of whom? To whom shall we give account? Give scriptures.
3. Who is the one mediator between God and man? Name some traits of this mediator.
4. Who are our ultimate examples of giving? Describe the sacrifices made by each.
5. Discuss our pattern for giving and our attitude as we give.
6. We give as we have purposed on the first day of the week for the work of the body of Christ. Does this end our responsibility of giving?
7. What great lessons do the parable of the talents teach?
8. What group of Christians was commended by Paul because they first gave themselves to the Lord?
9. In 2 Corinthians 8:7 what grace does Paul exhort them to abound in also?
10. How do we prove our love to our Father?
11. Describe the attitude of Ananias and Sapphira. From this event what do we learn about God's knowledge of the thoughts and intents of our hearts?
12. What was the fate of the rich fool who had plans to take it easy—to eat, drink, and be merry?
13. Describe the heart of the young rich man whom Jesus told to sell all his possessions. Why was this command given to him?
14. What instruction does Paul give the rich that they may inherit eternal life?
15. What was the gift Dorcas gave?
16. Describe the home of Mary, Martha, and Lazarus. What great lesson did Jesus teach in this home?
17. Would we open our homes more if we were not cumbered with many things?
18. Write your goal for improving your stewardship of what God has entrusted to you.

The Fruit of Our Lips

Jane McWhorter

Jane was born and reared in the Nashville, Tennessee, area and is a graduate of David Lipscomb University. She received her master's degree from Jacksonville State University and has done additional graduate work at the University of Alabama.

She is married to Don McWhorter, a minister of the church of Christ in Fayette, Alabama, since 1974. Jane and Don have two children, Kathy and Greg, and two grandchildren.

Jane is best known for her writing, lectures, and seminars. She is the author of several well-known books: *She Hath Done What She Could* (1973), *Caterpillars or Butterflies* (1977), Let This Cup Pass (1979), *Meet My Friend David* (1982), *Now I Can Fly* (1986), *Living Together in Knowledge* (1988) co-authored with Don, and *Friendship: Handle with Care* (1999).

Jane's speaking engagements have carried her throughout the brotherhood. She has been a speaker at six Christian colleges in addition to devoting much of her time to ladies' day programs, retreats, and workshops in twenty states as well as some of the Caribbean islands.

She taught school in Gadsden, Alabama, and Chattanooga, Tennessee, before moving to Fayette, where she taught the first grade for seventeen years. In 1987 she was one of eight teachers honored by the State of Alabama as *Elementary Teacher of the Year.* In 1990 the Pilot Club named Jane *Outstanding Handicapped Professional Woman in the State of Alabama.* In 1993 she was awarded the honor of being Alabama's *Mother of the Year.*

Jane is now retired from teaching school and devotes her time to serving God by her husband's side.

Joyful Noise

Since the dawn of civilization, mankind has used music as a means of giving expression to intangible feelings. Sorrow, happiness, love, frustration, praise to a higher being—all have found their places among the different races and in every period of time. God's people are no exception.

Most of us have smatterings of knowledge regarding the kind of music used in the Old Testament, but few Christians have any real, in-depth grasp of the overall picture. When we are asked why we do not worship God with mechanical instruments of music, how many times do we simply reply that we are no longer ruled by the laws of the Old Testament, when we really have little knowledge of what those laws were? Also, could we distinguish which Old Testament worship we are talking about? Was there more singing or more playing on mechanical instruments during that time? Does every mention of music imply it was done in worship? Do we understand the context of each reference? I invite you to take a fascinating journey through the scriptures to gain a deeper insight into the kind of music found in the Old Testament.

Patriarchal Age

As recorded in the first book of the Bible, God's people paid homage to him primarily by means of burnt offerings. Then, as now, Jehovah told his children what he required in worship. Abel had respect for God's specifications for a burnt offering (Heb. 11:4; Rom. 10:17) and was pleasing to him whereas Cain was not (Gen. 4:1-8). When God told Abraham to offer Isaac as a sacrifice, the word *worship* was used for the first time: "Abide ye here with the ass; and I and the lad will go yonder and worship, and come again to you" (Gen. 22:5).

By way of summary, we could say that the people worshiped by sacrificing. God talked directly with the patriarch of each family to make his wishes known.

The first mention of music in the Old Testament may be found in Genesis 4:21: "And his brother's name was Jubal: he was the father of all such as handle the harp and organ." Jubal was in the sixth generation from Cain. Adam Clark says, "It is very likely that both words are generic, the former including under it all stringed instruments, and the latter, all wind instruments."[1] The previous generations were merely listed, but the sons of Lamech were named with their accomplishments. Nothing is mentioned in this verse to imply Jubal's music was used in worship. (In this passage of *firsts,* it should be noted that Lamech, Jubal's father, was also a *first*—the first recorded incidence of a man's having more than one wife.)

Some musical instruments were simply a means of calling the people together.

At this point in our survey of music in the Old Testament, it would be wise to note that some music could be classified as secular. (This would include folklore songs as well as music used for entertainment, celebrations, weddings, and funerals.) Other music was used for worship. Some musical instruments were simply a means of calling the people together—a signal or summons. An understanding of these different types of music is important in our study.

After the mention of the name of Jubal as being the father of musical instruments, the next account of music is found in Genesis 31:27: "Wherefore didst thou flee away secretly, and steal away from me; and didst not tell me, that I might have sent thee away with mirth, and with songs, with tabret, and with harp." Laban was simply saying that he would have had a big celebration for Jacob, complete with musical instruments, if Jacob had only told his father-in-law that he was leaving. This passage has nothing to do with worship. It was merely a means of honoring departing guests—a going-away party.

---

1. Adam Clark, *Clark's Commentary* (New York, NY: Abingdon-Cokesbury Press, n.d.), vol. 2, p. 62.

The first fourteen chapters of Exodus are filled with the details of the deliverance of the children of Israel from the land of Egypt. Exodus 15:1-19 contains the words of a song that Moses and the sons of Israel sang unto the Lord after safely crossing the Red Sea. No instruments of music are mentioned. The text could suggest that only Moses and the other male leaders sang this song. At the conclusion of the song of Moses, his sister, Miriam, took a timbrel in her hand and led the women in dancing and in singing a song of praise to God for their miraculous deliverance (Exod. 15:20-21).

Later, in 1 Samuel 18:6-7, a similar celebration may be found. When David killed Goliath, the women met Saul and David with singing, dancing, tabrets, and with instruments of music. Percussion instruments, such as tabrets and timbrels, were used on festive occasions: "It is not mentioned in connection with divine service. It was generally played by women, and marked the time at dances or processions."[2]

Early Life of Moses

Three months after the exodus from Egypt, a trumpet was mentioned in connection with the command for Moses to sanctify the people in preparation for God's coming down on Mount Sinai in the sight of all the people. They were also summoned to the mountain by the trumpet. On the third day the trumpet sounded long and loud before Moses was called up into the mountain to receive the commands of God (Exod. 19:1-25).

> ***Two silver trumpets were to be blown only by the priests.***

Both trumpets and rams' horns in early Jewish history were used for signaling and announcing—not for playing melodies. Later, in Numbers 10:1-10, God gave Moses specific instructions regarding the use of two silver trumpets that were to be blown only by the priests—the two sons of Aaron at that time. Not intended for music, these instruments primarily were used to summon the people, tell them when to march and when to stop, give the call to battle, and announce religious observances. Because

2. *The International Standard Bible Encyclopedia* (Grand Rapids, MI: Wm. B. Eerdmans Publishing Co., 1960), vol. 3, p. 2101.

there were 600,000 men on foot (besides the children) when the Israelites left Egypt (Exod. 12:37)—and this number had grown substantially—more than just a human voice was needed to keep the people together as a unified whole. "Even in the Roman era, trumpet-like instruments, though prominent in art and literature, are not known to have been used in music. They remained instruments of only a few tones for signaling, announcing, commanding and ceremonial purposes."[3]

While Moses was on the mountain, singing was mentioned; but it was used in idol worship in connection with the golden calf and was accompanied by dancing around the newly made idol (Exod. 32:15-19).

Instructions for the Tabernacle

Instructions for the tabernacle were given in great detail in the remainder of the book of Exodus, but God made no provision for mechanical instruments of music in tabernacle worship. *The International Standard Bible Encyclopedia* states: "It is true that nothing is said of it [music] in the Pentateuch in connection with the consecration of the tabernacle, or the institution of the various sacrifices or festivals."[4] *Davis Dictionary of the Bible* adds: "It is not mentioned as belonging to the service of the tabernacle in the early period."[5]

There was no music provided in the tabernacle worship at all.

Adam Clark joined with the other authorities in asserting the absence of instrumental music in the original tabernacle plan for worship when he wrote, "Moses had not appointed any musical instruments to be used in the divine worship; there was nothing of the kind under the first tabernacle."[6]

In fact, there was no music provided in the tabernacle worship at all—neither vocal nor mechanical. The worship scene at

---

3. Don Michael Randel, *The New Harvard Dictionary of Music* (Cambridge, MA: Harvard University Press, 1986), p. 880.

4. *The International Standard Bible Encyclopedia,* vol. 3, p. 2095

5. John D. Davis, *Davis Dictionary of the Bible* (Grand Rapids, MI: Baker Book House, 1973), p. 544.

6. Clark, vol. 2, p. 690.

the tabernacle was so quiet that the tiny bells on the hem of Aaron's clothing were audible when he went into the holy place (Exod. 28:33-35). Music would not be introduced into tabernacle worship until the time of King David.

Music During the Time of the Judges

During the time of the judges, little was written about music. In the fifth chapter of Judges, Deborah's song of praise is recorded, but there is no mention of mechanical instruments.

In 1 Samuel 10:1-10 a psaltery, a tabret, and a pipe are mentioned. After telling Saul that he was God's choice to become the first king, Samuel gave Saul three signs to prove that his words were from God. The third sign involved Saul's meeting a group of prophets with musical instruments as they were prophesying. Saul himself would then begin to prophesy. These words were given as a sign to Saul, not as an example of divinely approved worship. The psaltery, tabret, and pipe were used as an indication that these were the men Samuel was talking about.

The Innovations of David

Exact chronologies are difficult to give. Because Paul stated the time frame for the period of the judges to be 450 years (Acts 13:20), it would be safe to assume that more than five hundred years had elapsed between the giving of the law and the ascension of David to the throne. After this long period of time, the new king introduced some dramatic additions to the Jewish worship. First Chronicles 23:5 speaks of four thousand Levites praising the Lord with the instruments which David had made. In a verse dealing with a later period of time, the use of mechanical instruments of music is again credited to the commandment of David (2 Chron. 29:25). Under the reign of King Josiah, the special singers used at the Passover traced their origin back to a much earlier commandment given by David (2 Chron. 35:15). Based upon these passages, there can be no doubt concerning the origin of music in the worship of the tabernacle. It originated with David. His innovations greatly influenced Jewish worship from approximately 1000 B.C. until the destruction of

The new king introduced some dramatic additions to the Jewish worship.

the temple in Jerusalem in A.D. 70. Probably the shepherd king's love of music prompted his actions. In 2 Samuel 23:1 he was called the sweet singer of Israel. David also played skillfully on the harp (1 Sam. 16:18-23; 2 Sam. 6:5). It was his reputation as a musician that secured for him the court position of soothing the nerves of King Saul with music.

The earliest mention of the special singers and mechanical instrumental music that were introduced into tabernacle worship by David centered around the moving of the ark of the covenant to Jerusalem after he had been crowned king over all Judah and Israel. (The ark had been captured by the Philistines in battle during the time of Eli but was soon returned to Hebrew territory. It stayed in Beth-shemesh in Gibeah at the house of Abinadab for twenty years, and then in Perez-uzzah at the house of Obededom for three months after Uzzah was killed by God for touching the ark when the oxen stumbled.)

The ark's final return to Jerusalem to a tent that David had prepared was quite a procession with harps, psalteries, timbrels, cornets, cymbals, trumpets, sacrifices, shouting, leaping, and dancing (2 Sam. 6:1-15; 1 Chron. 15:28). First Chronicles 15:19-22 outlined the organization of all the musicians in this entourage. David appointed Levites "to be singers with instruments of music, psalteries and harps and cymbals sounding, by lifting up the voice with joy" (1 Chron. 15:16). Three men—Heman, Asaph, and Ethan (Jeduthun)—were appointed to oversee the music. Chenaniah, chief of the Levites, was in charge of the singing (1 Chron. 15:17-24).

The celebration involved in the moving of the ark of the covenant to Zion seemed to be the reason for the formation of the Levite musicians and singers by David, but their use continued. The group under the direction of Asaph remained at the city of David to minister before the ark continually at the new tabernacle (1 Chron. 16:4-6, 37), but the two groups under the direction of Heman and Jeduthun were assigned to the old tabernacle at Gibeon (1 Chron. 16:37-42). "Hence it was that there were now two tabernacles, the original one with its altar at Gibeon and the new one with the original ark in Jerus, both under the protection of the king."[7]

---

7. *The International Standard Bible Encyclopedia,* vol. 5, p. 2892.

The three musical groups formed by King David were quite elaborate. The entire twenty-fifth chapter of 1 Chronicles is devoted to the number and offices of the singers and players. *Davis Dictionary of the Bible* summarizes the scope and duties of these musicians as follows:

> In David's reign they numbered 4000 (1 Chron. 23:5), of whom 288 were trained musicians, who were depended upon to lead the less skilled body of assistants (2 Chron. 25:7-8). They were divided into twenty-four courses, containing twelve trained musicians each. Of these courses four belonged to the family of Asaph, six to that of Jeduthun, and fourteen to that of Heman. The orchestra which accompanied the singing consisted of stringed instruments, but cymbals were also used, being probably struck by the chief musician to beat time (1 Chron. 15:10-20). It appears from this passage that the proportion of psalteries to harps was eight to six.[8]

Only designated Levites played, and the musical instruments were harps, lyres, and cymbals—instruments that allowed the player to sing and play at the same time. The singing was done by the designated Levites. The magnitude of the book of Psalms attests to the fact that singing was the most important part of the musical work in the tabernacle and temple.

The temple, along with its worship, was to appeal to the senses of men.

Because King David had shed much blood, he was denied the right to build the temple (1 Chron. 22:8). Although he could not actually construct the building, he made great preparations for it before he died. He wanted the building to be "exceeding magnificent, of fame and glory throughout all countries" (1 Chron. 22:5). The temple, along with its worship, was to appeal to the senses of men.

Part of David's last wishes related to plans for the continuation of the musicians he had initiated (1 Chron. 24:1-31). After David's death, when Solomon had reigned for four years, the new king began the construction of the magnificent temple. When it was completed, according to the wishes of David, elaborate music had a part in this magnificent building.

After King Solomon had the ark brought into the temple, the priests came out of the Holy Place. Then the Levites, who were the singers, stood at the east end of the altar with cymbals, psal-

8. Davis, p. 544.

teries, and harps. The 120 trumpets were sounded by the priests, and the Levites lifted up their voices with the instruments of music and praised the Lord (2 Chron. 5:11-13).

Music after the Death of Solomon

After the death of Solomon and the division of the kingdom, the temple ceased to be the one place of worship. Calves of gold were erected at Bethel and Dan as the nation began to be led away into idolatry (1 Kings 12:27-31). Wars raged and the people's interest in spiritual matters waned. Gradually the temple was plundered and depleted as kings tried to use its treasures to secure the assistance of foreign countries.

Approximately three hundred years after the death of David, King Hezekiah, who reigned from 715-686 B.C., is credited with much temple repair and also for trying to restore temple worship. He carried on David's tradition by restoring the singers and the instruments ordained by David (2 Chron. 29:25-30). Restoration also occurred under the reign of King Josiah (2 Chron. 34:12; 35:15). After approximately four hundred years, the temple was completely destroyed by the plundering Babylonian army when Nebuchadnezzar carried the Israelites into captivity (2 Kings 25:8-9).

Second Chronicles 29:25

At this point it would be wise to consider a verse written concerning the reign of King Hezekiah. It is sometimes cited as proof that musical instruments in worship were authorized by the commandment of God:

> And he set the Levites in the house of the Lord with cymbals, with psalteries, and with harps, according to the commandment of David, and of Gad the king's seer, and Nathan the prophet: for so was the commandment of the Lord by his prophets (2 Chron. 29:25).

In one of the replies of Guy N. Woods at the open forum at Freed Hardeman College, he made the following comments concerning this verse:

> We have earlier observed that, again and again, the cymbals, psalteries, and harps were said to have been introduced by the commandment of David: and, such is affirmed here. Moreover, it should be observed that two actions are contemplated for which there were two different com-

mandments: (1) the commandment of Jehovah for the installation of the Levites; (2) the commandment of David involving the use of the cymbals, psalteries, and musical instruments. Neither here, nor elsewhere, in the sacred writings, is God said to have commanded such activity in his worship.

Concerning 2 Chronicles 29:25, Adam Clark observed:

It was by the hand or commandment of the Lord and his prophets that the Levites should praise the Lord; for so the Hebrew text may be understood; and it was by the order of David that so many instruments of music should be introduced into the divine service. But were it even evident, which it is not, either from this place or any other place in the sacred writings, that instruments of music were prescribed by divine authority under the law, could this be adduced with any semblance of reason, that they ought to be used in Christian worship? No: the whole spirit, soul, and genius of the Christian religion are against this: and those who know the Church of God best, and what constitutes its genuine spiritual state, know that these things have been introduced as a substitute for the life and power of religion; and that where they prevail most, there is least of the power of Christianity.[9]

Neither should it be inferred from this passage that the instruments were placed in the Holy Place just because the words "in the house of the Lord" are used. Those same words were used in the next chapter in reference to the outer court (2 Chron. 30:15).

Psalms

It was during the time of David that the book of Psalms was written. It was a collection of religious poems used by the Israelites, and a great many of them were written by David himself. "Seventy-three psalms are designated David's in their Hebrew titles; and as in many cases the intention is to indicate that he is the author."[10] Undoubtedly music was an integral part of the young shepherd's life because he already had a reputation for playing well on the harp when he was first mentioned in the scriptures (1 Sam. 16:14-23). His love of music probably began when he was watching his sheep on the lonely hills and continued to be a solace during the ten years of running from Saul, as well as throughout his trials and happy times during the

It was a collection of religious poems used by the Israelites.

9. Clark, vol. 2, p. 690.

10. Davis, p. 174-175.

remainder of his life. A perusal of the book of Psalms exposes other familiar names: sons of Korah (Heman, the singer, was a son of Korah), Asaph, Ethan, and others. David introduced the use of these psalms into the tabernacle, and they were continued throughout Jewish history. The combination of singing and playing mechanical instruments of music may be seen in the following passages:

- "Praise the Lord with harp: sing unto him with the psaltery and an instrument of ten strings" (Ps. 33:2).
- "I will sing and give praise . . . awake, psaltery and harp" (Ps. 57:7-8).
- "The singers went before, the players on instruments followed after" (Ps. 68:25).
- "I will also praise thee with the psaltery . . . unto thee will I sing with the harp" (Ps. 71:22).
- "Sing aloud unto God our strength: make a joyful noise unto the God of Jacob. Take a psalm, and bring hither the timbrel, the pleasant harp with the psaltery" (Ps. 81:1-2).
- "As well the singers as the players on instruments shall be there" (Ps. 87:7).
- "It is a good thing to give thanks unto the Lord, and to sing praises unto thy name, O Most High: to show forth thy loving-kindness in the morning, and the faithfulness every night, upon an instrument of ten strings, and upon the psaltery; upon the harp with a solemn sound" (Ps. 92:1-3).
- "Sing unto the Lord with the harp; with harp, and the voice of a psalm. With trumpets and sound of cornet make a joyful noise before the Lord the King" (Ps. 98:5-6).
- "Let them praise his name in the dance: let them sing praises unto him with the timbrel and harp" (Ps. 149:3).
- "Praise him with the sound of the trumpet: praise him with the psaltery and harp. Praise him with the timbrel and dance: praise him with stringed instruments and organs. Praise him upon the loud cymbals: praise him upon the high sounding cymbals" (Ps. 150:3-5).

The Second Temple

When the Babylonian Empire fell to the Persians, Cyrus, the Persian ruler, ordered the return of the Jews and also the rebuilding of the temple at Jerusalem under the direction of Zerubbabel. After the builders laid the foundation, the Levites sang praises and used cymbals to praise the Lord, "after the ordinance of David, king of Israel" (Ezra 3:10-11). When the new walls surrounding Jerusalem were dedicated, there were singers and musical instruments in the celebration (Neh. 12:27-28). The musical part of their religious activities continued to be under the direction of the Levites and the priests continued to sound the trumpets. Nehemiah 12:47 states that a portion of the daily sacrifices were given to the singers. Other passages written during this period of time indicate that there was a group of singers who did not play instruments (Ezra 2:70; Neh. 7:73; 10:28; 12:28).

A portion of the daily sacrifices were given to the singers.

Secular history expands upon the embellishments of later musical programs in the temple. *Davis Dictionary of the Bible* adds the following description of events associated with the Feast of the Tabernacles:

> It was also customary in the evening following the first day of the festival, and perhaps on the subsequent evenings, to illuminate the court of the women from two lofty stands, each supporting four immense lamps, which threw their light not only into the courts of the temple, but far and wide over the city. The wicks were made of the cast-off linens of the priests. Levites, stationed on the steps of the court, rendered instrumental music and sang psalms; and a dance was performed by prominent laymen and priests.[11]

Did God Command the Use of Instrumental Music in Old Testament Worship?

There is no doubt but that David added the use of instrumental music and special choral groups to religious observances. They were not given as commands at the inception of the tabernacle worship and apparently were not used on the premises for worship for more than five hundred years until after the time when David used them in the celebration of returning the ark of the covenant to Jerusalem. He then authorized the continuation of their use. (Remember, at the beginning of tabernacle worship, the priests were commanded to use silver trumpets to summon

---

11. Davis, p. 801.

the people and to announce special events, but the instruments were not part of the worship.)

Over and over, throughout the pages of the Old Testament, David alone was given credit for introducing his system of praising God by his musical innovations (1 Chron. 23:5; 2 Chron. 7:6; 229:26-27; 35:15; Ezra 3:10-11).

It would certainly appear that God simply tolerated David's special music in worship.

From all the evidence found in this study, it would certainly appear that God simply tolerated David's special music in worship. Originally musical instruments were not used in any part of the tabernacle for worship, and the condition remained that way for hundreds of years. Although they were used in the court by the brazen altar in David's time and thereafter, even then they still were not used in the Most Holy Place nor the Holy Place, which was a pattern for the Lord's church yet to come (Heb. 9:1-29). Only the family of Aaron could enter the Holy Place and only the High Priest could make the annual entrance into the Most Holy Place (Exod. 30:17-21, 29-30). The musicians were from the ranks of the Levites, not the priestly line of Aaron and his sons, and they were not permitted to enter either of these places (Heb. 9:6-7).

Three Other Instances of Man's Innovations That Were Tolerated By God

(1) *At the beginning of civilization, Jehovah's plan for marriage was monogamy* (Gen. 2:18-24). The first recorded instance of multiple wives was that of Lemech, fifth generation from Cain and the father of Jubal, who invented musical instruments (Gen. 4:19). Abraham, Jacob, David, Solomon, and most of God's other leaders during the Patriarchal and Mosaical times had multiple wives, and even concubines. (Solomon had seven hundred wives and three hundred concubines, many of whom were from other nations: a practice that had been forbidden by God [1 Kings 11:1-3; Exod. 34:16; Deut. 7:1-5]). God tolerated this deviation from his original plan.

(2) *From the beginning Jehovah did not favor divorce, but concessions were made because of the hardness of the hearts of his people* (Matt. 19:3-9; Mark 10:2-9). Deuteronomy 24:1-4 gave guidelines, but the practice of divorce became more and more accepted by the people. "Divorces from the earliest times were common among the Hebrews."[12] In the New Testament Christ restated God's original intent—one man and one woman joined together as long as they both live. Only one exception was given for divorce and remarriage while one's partner was alive: adultery. The innocent party then has the right to put the guilty one away and remarry.

(3) *God tolerated a king for the Israelites, but it was not his desire*. His original plan was to rule over his people himself. The Israelites became dissatisfied and desired to make Gideon a king and have his sons succeed him, but Gideon refused because he knew that it was not God's will (Judg. 8:22-23). Time elapsed and the same wish surfaced during the lifetime of Samuel and his wayward sons. The people wanted a king like the nations around them (1 Sam. 8:4-7). God warned them, through Samuel, about the consequences of having an earthly king; but they still clamored for one. "And the Lord said to Samuel, Hearken unto their voice, and make them a king" (1 Sam. 8:22). God did not want his people to have kings, but he tolerated the practice and even played a part in their selection throughout the years.

The people wanted a king like the nations around them.

Conclusions

A new day was approaching. The law served as a schoolmaster to bring God's children to Christ. "But after that faith is come, we are no longer under a schoolmaster" (Gal. 3:25). The different items in the tabernacle were types or patterns of things yet to come, but a better system of worship was approaching (Heb. 9:1-10:39).

---

12. *The International Standard Bible Encyclopedia,* vol. 2, p. 864.

Because Christ would one day make the supreme sacrifice, there would then no longer be a need for daily burnt offerings. There would be no more priests in elegant robes. Every child of God, even in the humblest of clothes, would serve in this office. A time would come when the ceremonial cleansing would be replaced by baptism. No longer would incense be offered before the throne of God. Each Christian would be able to pour out his heart to the Almighty in prayer through the intercession of the slain Lamb. Instead of the eating of shewbread by the priests, every child of God would have the privilege of partaking of the Lord's supper each Sunday. Gone would be the circumcision of the flesh. Houses, and sometimes even caves, would replace the majestic temple with all its costly splendor.

A time would come when the ceremonial cleansing would be replaced by baptism.

Things God had previously tolerated—but not desired—would also be gone. No longer would he tolerate divorces or multiple wives. Earthly kings would be replaced by the divine King of kings. Changes were also in store for the music he had tolerated. Gone would be the instruments of music. Gone would be the elaborate choral groups of Levites, who stood in the court of the temple and put on a spectacular performance for the people to enjoy. Gone would be the dancing that often accompanied the music.

Under the new system, music would come from the hearts of all Christians as they poured out their words of worship to the Almighty. Under the new law, the instruments to be played would be the strings of their hearts. Nothing else would be needed. Their entire lives would be living sacrifices. It would be better.

Questions

1. During the Patriarchal Age, what was the primary method of worship?
2. Where is the first mention of music in the Old Testament? Under what circumstances was it mentioned?
3. Trace the use of music in the books of Genesis and Exodus.
4. If Miriam's song of praise with the timbrel after the crossing of the Red Sea can be used to defend mechanical instruments of music in worship, what can be said of her dancing?

5. Discuss the different items used in connection with worship in the tabernacle. Was there any provision for mechanical instruments of music? What about the silver trumpets? Who used them and for what purpose?
6. What innovations did David add to the worship? How did they have their beginning?
7. Describe the musical groups instigated by David. For how long were they continued?
8. Did God command the use of instrumental music in Old Testament worship? Did he tolerate it? What is the difference?
9. Cite at least three other examples of God's toleration of practices he had not commanded.
10. Can 2 Chronicles 29:25-30 be used to prove that mechanical instruments of music in worship were introduced by the commandment of God? Defend your answer.
11. When the Old Testament closed, a new covenant was approaching. It provided for a different method of worshipping the Almighty. How was the worship to be different? What was the impact upon music in worship?

The Fruit of Our Lips
New Testament

Heart Song

Multitudes of people had flocked to Jerusalem for the Passover that week. Thousands of lambs had been slaughtered at the impressive temple amid elaborate pageantry. Outside the city gates on a hillside called Calvary, however, the supreme sacrifice was being offered. No more scapegoats would annually bear sins to a distant, isolated land (Lev. 16:6-10). The perfect Lamb, without spot or blemish, was being offered—not on an elaborate brazen altar in a temple but on a rugged cross situated on a lonely hillside. There was one last cry: It is finished! (John 19:30.) One last breath, and then it was all over.

The Son of God had accomplished his mission: he had fulfilled the law (Matt. 5:17-18). The previous covenant, made between God and his selected people, had been nailed to the cross (Col. 2:14). The older law had been faulty (Heb. 8:7), but it served as a schoolmaster (a tutor) to bring the Jews to Christ (Gal. 3:24). From the very beginning God intended for his covenant with the Israelites to be temporary (Gal. 3:19), but the first covenant had been "a shadow of the good things to come" (Heb. 10:1).

Those good things to come, spoken of by the writer of Hebrews, were unveiled fifty days later on the occasion of another important Jewish celebration—Pentecost—when multitudes of people had again gathered in Jerusalem. Peter preached the first gospel sermon and the church was established when three thousand souls were baptized (Acts 2:41).

No longer was worship required at an elaborate edifice. The early Christians met in homes or wherever they could find a place to assemble. There were to be no more bloody sacrifices. The supreme sacrifice had been paid once and for all. Worship under the new covenant was to be different. Only two tangible things were required: unleavened bread and the fruit of the vine, which were commonly available. No longer was incense needed. The prayers of the most humble Christians could now find their way to the throne of God through the intercession of the sacrificed Lamb. The music was also to be different.

Music in the Church of the First Century

Although God had made no provisions for musical instruments to be used in the worship at the original tabernacle, and they had been absent for over five hundred years, David introduced and promoted them. Their continued use was found in the worship under other kings. Elaborate choral groups were also a part of temple worship. (Note the previous chapter concerning music in the Old Testament.) God supposedly tolerated these practices.

A simple, heartfelt religion was to replace the pomp and pageantry of the temple.

The death of Christ did away with the Mosaical Law with all its hundreds of rules and regulations. The new covenant was to be different. A simple, heartfelt religion was to replace the pomp and pageantry of the temple. Hopefully, the people had matured spiritually to the point that they themselves could come wholeheartedly before the throne of God, realizing that he was the one to be praised in the manner of his choice whether they understood his reasons or not. The people were now to be participants instead of spectators.

Because the new covenant with God's people was not itemized in a long list of things to do or not to do, we must now find his plan by searching his word. Christians of the first century were guided by the miraculous manifestations of the Holy Spirit in determining the will of God. With the completion of the written word, this stage of the infancy of the church passed and so did the miraculous guidance (1 Cor. 13:8-10; James 1:25). Today the only way Christians can know what God expects of them is to turn to the pages of inspiration. There must be a divine command, an approved example, or a necessary implication for all that we do. We must also respect the silence of the scriptures.

A Search of New Testament Scriptures

Mechanical instruments of music are found within the pages of the New Testament, but there is no indication they were used for religious purposes (Matt. 6:2; 9:23; 11:17; 24:31; Luke 7:32; 15:25; 1 Cor. 13:1; 14:7-8; 15:52; 1 Thess. 4:16; Heb. 12:19). Because the book of Revelation is a prophesy concerning future events, both the instruments and the singing will be considered later in this lesson.

A perusal of the New Testament scriptures finds the following instances of singing. With the exception of Ephesians 5:19 and Colossians 3:16, often these verses are simply mentioned in a Bible class involving a discussion of music in the New Testament. All too often little is said concerning the context in which they are found.

(1) Matthew 26:30—The first account is in the context of the institution of the Lord's supper in the upper room after Christ and his apostles had celebrated the Passover. "And when they had sung a hymn, they went out into the mount of Olives." Although this instance is found under the covers of the New Testament, it actually occurred under the Mosaical Law because it happened before the old law was abolished.

(2) Mark 14:26—"And when they had sung an hymn, they went out into the mount of Olives." This verse is a parallel passage to Matthew 26:30 and has the same context.

(3) Acts 16:25—"And at midnight Paul and Silas prayed and sang praises unto God: and the prisoners heard them." These two Christians found themselves badly beaten and in prison for doing the will of God by casting an evil spirit from a young girl. They undoubtedly sought spiritual strength by singing hymns of praise and by praying to the one who had the power to deliver them.

(4) Romans 15:8-9—"Now I say that Jesus Christ was a minister of the circumcision for the truth of God, to confirm the promises made unto the fathers: and that the Gentiles might glorify God for his mercy; as it is written, For this cause I will confess to thee among the Gentiles, and sing unto thy name." The context of this passage was an effort made by Paul to reconcile Jewish and Gentile Christians in religious fellowship. Just as the Jews had a right to glorify God for his

truth, so did the Gentiles have a right to glorify God for his mercy. Paul substantiated his assertion by quoting Psalm 18:49 to prove that the Gentiles also had a right to hope.

(5) 1 Corinthians 14:15—"What is it then: I will pray with the spirit, and I will pray with the understanding also: I will sing with the spirit, and I will sing with the understanding also." This verse is surrounded by instructions for edifying the church while the miraculous gifts of prophesying and speaking in tongues—a foreign language unknown to the speaker—were being exercised. Although the age of miracles ceased when the Bible was completely written, the thrust of verses 16-19 is applicable today. Just as Christians at Corinth were admonished to pray and sing in a language that could be understood by all, so should our praying and singing be done in an understandable manner for the edification of those assembled (1 Cor. 14:18-19).

Our praying and singing should be done in an understandable manner for edification.

(6) Ephesians 5:19—"Speaking to yourselves in psalms and hymns and spiritual songs, singing and making melody in your heart to the Lord." The book of Ephesians was written by Paul and was directed to the members of the Lord's church at Ephesus. This particular verse is within the general context of exhortations to Christian living. In the immediate context a distinction was being made between the behavior of God's children and that of unbelievers. The contrasting wisdom and the folly of the two groups is reflected in the (1) wise use of time (v. 16), (2) the desire to learn God's will and understand it (v. 17), in addition to (3) being filled with the things of the Spirit instead of being filled with wine (v. 18). Being filled with the Spirit refers to one who minds the things of the Spirit. Spirit-filled people were then admonished to do the following things:

a. *"Speaking"*—The Greek word for speaking is *laleo* and means "to utter or form words with the mouth, to speak."[1] Consequently, the music described in this verse must be in words.

---

1. Joseph Henry Thayer, *A Greek-English Lexicon of the New Testament* (Grand Rapids, MI: Baker Book House, 1977), p. 368.

b. *"To yourselves"*—The singing had to be reciprocal; the Ephesian Christians were commanded to sing to one another. Because this epistle was directed to every member (Eph. 1:1), each one would be expected to sing. Only congregational singing, in which everyone sings, would be acceptable.
c. *"In psalms, and hymns, and spiritual songs"*—Without going into a lengthy discussion of the nuances of meanings in the three types of acceptable songs, the concise meanings of these words are used as they appeared in an editorial written by Glenn Colley in *Words of Truth*:

> This describes the lyrics of approved music. Psalms are scripture set to music. Hymns are songs of praise to God. Spiritual songs describe those which are designed around spiritual themes and which motivate singers and listeners to greater spiritual service.[2]

d. *"Singing"*—"Singing" is from the word *ado* meaning "to sing." "It is used always of praise to God."[3]
e. *"And making melody"*—"Making melody" is from *psallo* and is defined in New Testament usage as "to sing a hymn, sing praise."[4] (A more detailed discussion of *psallo* is presented later in this chapter.)
f. *"In your heart to the Lord"*—"Heart" comes from the word *kardia* and refers to the "thoughts or feelings (mind)."[5] "Making melody" must involve the feelings of the inward person as well as audible words of praise.

(7) Colossians 3:16—"Let the word of Christ dwell in you richly in all wisdom; teaching and admonishing one another in psalms and hymns and spiritual songs, singing with grace in your hearts to the Lord." Paul's admonition to the church in Colosse is parallel to his words in Ephesians 5:19. It is given in the context of a description of the former state of these Christians (vv. 7-9) and an admonition to remember

---

2. Glenn Colley, "Special Music in the Church—Ephesians 5:19," *Words of Truth* (Jasper, AL: Sixth Avenue Church of Christ), vol. 34, no. 48, p. 2.

3. W. E. Vine, Merrill F. Unger, William White, Jr., *Vine's Expository Dictionary of Biblical Words* (Nashville, TN: Thomas Nelson Publishers, 1985), p. 578.

4. Vine, p. 402.

5. James Strong, *The New Strong's Exhaustive Concordance of the Bible* (Nashville, TN: Thomas Nelson Publishers, 1984), p. 39.

that there should no longer be Greek or Jew, circumcision or uncircumcision (v. 11). After listing the attributes they should possess, Paul then taught the Colossian Christians:

a. *"Let the word of Christ dwell in you richly in all wisdom"*—The teachings of Christ were to dwell in them and eventually should produce wisdom as they learned more and more of his will. Today the only way Christians can know the word of Christ is by diligently studying the scriptures.
b. *"Teaching and admonishing one another"*—When the Colossian Christians knew the word of Christ, it was their duty to impart that knowledge to others and urge them to do what is right.
c. *"In psalms, and hymns, and spiritual songs"*—Paul gave the Colossians a method of teaching the word of Christ to others: by means of psalms, hymns, and spiritual songs. These three types of religious songs are the same listed in Ephesians 5:19. Singing in worship was to have a twofold purpose—praising God as well as teaching and admonishing one another. Truth cannot be taught by singing a song that has error in the words.

Truth cannot be taught by singing a song that has error in the words.

d. *"Singing with grace in your hearts to the Lord"*—The translation "singing" is from the same Greek word used in Ephesians 5:19: *ado.*

(8) Hebrews 2:12—"In the midst of the church will I sing praise unto thee." This verse is preceded by a discussion of the suffering of Christ and the sanctification of Christians through him. Paul quoted Psalm 22:22 as referring to Christ: "I will declare thy name unto my brethren: in the midst of the congregation will I praise thee."

(9) James 5:13—"Is any among you afflicted? let him pray. Is any merry? let him sing psalms." In this verse and the following one, James gave admonitions to people in three different circumstances. Those who were afflicted were to pray. Those who were merry were to sing. Those who were sick were to call for the elders to pray over them and care for them medically by the anointing of oil. The Greek word translated "sing" is *psallo* as used in 1 Corinthians 14:15; Romans 15:9; and Ephesians 5:19.

(10) Hebrews 13:15—"By him therefore let us offer the sacrifice of praise to God continually, that is, the fruit of our lips, giving thanks to his name." While this verse does not specify singing, some feel that it is implied because of the phrase, "the fruit of our lips."

A Christian's praise to God is to be made with his lips—his voice.

A Christian's praise to God is to be made with his lips—his voice—and not by a mechanical instrument of music. After the death of Christ, there were to be no more burnt offerings—only the living sacrifices of our lives.

Conclusions Drawn from the New Testament Examples and Commandments.

Thus far in this particular study, we have looked at every mention of the word *sing* or *singing* among Christians in the New Testament church. While some of the passages are incidental, we are told enough to know—without a doubt—that the singing of psalms, hymns, and spiritual songs was a part of the lives of those Christians. This truth is revealed both by divine commandments and approved examples. By stark contrast, there is not one hint of mechanical instruments of music being used in the church of the first century, either by themselves or in the sense of accompanying the human voice. In view of the fact that these people had been accustomed to elaborate performances of instrumental music during the time of King David and in the court of the temple thereafter, the implication of the silence of the scriptures is overwhelming. The new worship was to be different from the one to which they had grown accustomed. Now the musical praises were to be offered only by human voices.

Early Church History

After the last book of the Bible was written, mankind has not had a divinely inspired record of what happened to the church, but instead has had to rely upon historians. Although there is some variance in an exact date for the adoption of the use of mechanical instruments of music in worship, historians seem to agree that the date was several hundred years after the New Testament had been completed. Common sense tells anyone that there must have been some apparent reason for the absence of such instruments, as well as the objections to them, because both the Jewish and the Gentile converts to Christianity had been accustomed to some form of musical instruments, at least in the courts of their temples, for hundreds of years before the establishment of the church. The new practice of only singing was a drastic change in their previous practices. If the first-century church had used musical instruments in worship, then logically the practice would have continued into the second, third, and fourth centuries.

James W. McKinnon published his doctoral dissertation at Columbia University in 1965 on the subject, *The Church Fathers and Musical Instruments.* In this scholarly writing he revealed his research had shown not only that the early writers opposed the use of mechanical instruments of music but "they were not used in the patristic period."[6] He went on to state that, during this period of time, "the issue of instruments in church was never raised."[7] They were "a symbol of lasciviousness and debauchery."[8] Concerning the use of mechanical instruments of music, the evidence showed "that they were not used in the early Church."[9] This writer drew some conclusions about the introduction of the organ into the worship. "It appeared with some frequency during the period from 1000 to 1300 while in the later Middle Ages its use continued to spread until it was nearly universal."[10]

American Cyclopedia places the date of the introduction of the organ into church worship at an earlier date: "Pope Vitalian is related to have first introduced organs into some of the churches of Western Europe, about 670; but the earliest trustworthy account is that of one sent as a present by the Greek Emperor, Constantine Copronymus, to Pepin, king of the Franks, in 755."[11]

---

6. James W. McKinnon, *The Church Fathers and Musical Instruments* (Ph.D. Dissertation: Columbia University, 1965), p. 268.

7. Ibid., p. 263.

8. Ibid., p. 2.

9. Ibid., p. 264.

10. Ibid., p. 269.

11. *American Cyclopedia*, vol. 12, p. 688.

McClintock and Strong's Cyclopedia gives an earlier date and also notes that vocal music has always been used in the Eastern Church: "... which [sacred music] in the Eastern Church has never been any other than vocal, instrumental music being unknown in that church, as it was in the primitive Church. Students of ecclesiastical archaeology are generally agreed that instrumental music was not used in churches till after 600."[12]

... instrumental music was not used in churches till after 600.

Later Religious History

M. C. Kurfees, the author of *Instrumental Music in the Worship* (first published in 1911), quoted John Spencer Curwen, member of the Royal Academy of Music in London (ca. 1880): "Men still living can remember the time when organs were very seldom found outside the church of England. The Methodists, Independents, and Baptists rarely had them, and by the Presbyterians they were stoutly opposed."[13]

"I have no objections to instruments of music in our chapels, provided they are neither heard nor seen."

The thoughts of John Wesley (1703-1791), the founder of the Methodist Church, were preserved by Adam Clarke in his commentary on Amos 6:5: "I have no objections to instruments of music in our chapels, provided they are neither heard nor seen."[14]

David Benedict, a noted Baptist historian, wrote of the early view of the Baptists regarding the use of instruments in worship in his book, *Fifty Years Among the Baptists:*

> Staunch old Baptists in former times would as soon have tolerated the Pope of Rome in their pulpits as an organ in their galleries, and yet the instrument has gradually found its way among them, and their successors in church management, with nothing like the jars and difficulties

---

12. McClintock and Strong's Cyclopedia, vol. 8, p. 739.

13. M. C. Kurfees, *Instrumental Music in the Worship* (Nashville, TN; Gospel Advocate, 1950), p. 146.

14. Adam Clark, *Clark's Commentary* (New York, NY: Abingdon-Cokesbury Press, n.d.), vol. 3, p. 686.

which arose of old concerning the bass viol and smaller instruments of music.[15]

Restoration History

By way of summary, it can be said that all the evidence of early church historians supports the fact that, after the close of the pages of inspiration, Christians used no mechanical instruments of music in worship for hundreds of years. Later they were introduced against great opposition, and many of the earliest leaders of the Reformation were not in favor of the practice. The grassroots efforts of the Restoration Movement grew as men bravely abandoned the idea of trying to *reform* the Catholic Church and instead simply tried to restore to the New Testament pattern of church organization and worship. From the earliest days of the Restoration until the 1850s, mechanical instruments of music were not used in the worship of the Lord's church. The first well-documented use of the instrument was in Midway, Kentucky, under the leadership of L. L. Pinkerton in 1859.[16] The question concerning the use of instrumental music in worship, along with other problems, finally resulted in an open division of the church into two bodies. The existence of the division was acknowledged by David Lipscomb in 1907.[17]

Many of the earliest leaders of the Reformation were not in favor of the practice.

Psallo

Because some claim the Greek word *psallo* (found in four of the passages concerning singing) indicates the use of mechanical instruments of music, it is best to pause and examine the exact meanings of the words found in each of the passages quoted above.

(1) The Greek word *ado* (103) is found in these passages: Ephesians 5:19 and Colossians 3:16. The Greek word *humneo*

---

15. David Benedict, *Fifty Years Among the Baptists* (1859, reprint by Newman & Collins, 1913), p. 206.

16. J. E. Choate and William Woodson, *Sounding Brass and Clanging Cymbals* (Henderson, TN: Freed-Hardeman University, 1991), p. 21-22.

17. David Lipscomb, "The 'Churches of Christ' and the 'Disciples of Christ,'" *Gospel Advocate,* 44 (July 18, 1907), p. 457.

(5214) is found in the following verses: Matthew 26:30; Mark 14:26; Acts 16:25; Hebrews 2:12. Strong, Thayer, and Vine (all recognized authorities of the Greek language) agree that these words mean "sing." There is no problem involved in understanding the message.

(2) In Romans 15:9; 1 Corinthians 14:15; Ephesians 5:19; and James 5:13 the Greek word *psallo* (5567) is used. (Note that both *ado* 'singing' and *psallo* 'making melody' are used in Ephesians 5:19.)

A. Strong translates *psallo* as "to twitch or twang, i.e. to play on a stringed instrument; make melody; sing (psalms)."[18]

B. Vine gives the following definition of *psallo*: " 'to twitch, twang . . . to play a stringed instrument with the fingers,' and hence, in the Sept., 'to sing with a harp, sing psalms,' denotes in the NT, 'to sing a hymn, sing praise.' "[19]

C. Thayer defines *psallo* as "to touch or strike the chord, to twang the strings of a musical instrument so that they gently vibrate—to play on a stringed instrument, to play the harp, etc.—in the NT, to sing a hymn, to celebrate the praises of God in song."[20]

D. M. C. Kurfees in his book, *Instrumental Music in the Worship,* summarized the definitions of *psallo* during different periods of time from seventeen Greek-English lexicons as follows:

> To pluck the hair; (2) to twang the bowstring; (3) to twitch a carpenter's line; (4) to touch the chords of a musical instrument, that is, to make instrumental music; (5) to touch the chords of the human heart, that is, to sing, to celebrate with human praise.[21]

E. Note that the word *psallo* is translated "sing" in Romans 15:9; 1 Corinthians 14:15; and James 5:13. In Ephesians 5:19 *psallo* is translated "making melody" and is used along with *ado*, which is translated "sing."

F. These Greek authorities are in agreement that the word *psallo* means to touch the strings of an instrument—to

---

18. Strong, p. 78.
19. Vine, p. 402.
20. Thayer, p. 675.
21. Kurfees, p. 16.

make them vibrate—but *what* is touched is not found in *psallo*. Words often change in nuances of meaning through the years. Both Vine and Thayer state that in New Testament times *psallo* simply meant to sing a hymn, sing praise, celebrate the praises of God. Out of the four passages in which the word is used—Romans 15:9; 1 Corinthians 14:15; Ephesians 5:19; James 5:13—only Ephesians 5:19 reveals the instrument that is to be touched or plucked is the strings of the heart.

The instrument that is to be touched or plucked is the strings of the heart.

G. If *psallo* indicates the necessity of a mechanical instrument of music, then each person must play his own instrument as he sings and worships. Also, by the same reasoning, horns, trumpets, flutes, drums, cymbals, and all other mechanical instruments without strings could not be used in worship services.

"The Silence of the Scriptures" or "God Has Spoken"

Members of the Lord's church often talk about the "silence of the scriptures" in giving reasons for what should be excluded in the worship or organization of the church, but this term is not inclusive enough. The term "what God has authorized" better conveys the meaning.

There are two kind of commands in the scriptures: specific and generic. When God told Noah to make an ark of gopher wood, that command was specific and excluded any other kind of wood to be used in the building. If Jehovah had told Noah simply to use wood, then one kind of wood would have been just as good as any other. Some things were left to Noah's judgment. God did not tell him how to cut the wood nor how to get it to the building site. He did not tell Noah to use an ax or a saw nor how to measure it. In the generic command to "make thee an ark," matters of expediency in getting the vessel built were left to Noah's judgment. But God's specific command concerning the kind of wood to be used excluded all other wood simply because he had not authorized them but instead had authorized gopher wood.

If God had told New Testament Christians "to make music," that command would have been generic. Pianos, organs, harps, singing—all would be acceptable ways of making music. But his command was not generic. It was specific when he only authorized singing. Our question should be, "What kind of command did God authorize: generic or specific?"

"What kind of command did God authorize: generic or specific?"

Music in the Book of Revelation

Many who uphold the use of mechanical instruments of music in worship cite passages in the book of Revelation for support.

It must be remembered that Revelation is a book of prophecy and has nothing to do with the examples of worship in the church of the first century.

Trumpets are found in a number of verses in Revelation, but these instruments were used for signaling, not making melody.

Harps are mentioned several times, but so are golden bowls of incense (Rev. 5:8). Burning incense today would be just as binding as playing on a harp if we are going to take the book of Revelation as our guide for worship. Instead, it is a book of symbolic language. The inspired words of the account of the early church never hinted that first-century Christians ever played on harps in worship.

Special Music

Only one chapter in a book concerning New Testament music in worship does not allow an extended study of the use of special music in the worship, but it should be mentioned because of its propagation by some in the brotherhood.

Our modern culture demands that we be entertained. In keeping with the trend for entertainment, some brethren advocate a change in the way we worship God in music.

Lynn Anderson in his book, *Navigating the Winds of Change*, recommends that music used in worship be changed in two ways: musical idioms and musical formats.[22]

---

22. Lynn Anderson, *Navigating the Winds of Change* (West Monroe, LA: Howard Publishing Company, 1994), p. 124.

Musical *idioms* refer to the types of music such as traditional, classical, contemporary, or Stamps-Baxter. As long as the words in a song are true to Bible teaching, there is certainly nothing wrong with using new lyrics set to newer melodies. Neither is there anything wrong with projecting the words of the song on a large screen instead of reading them from a song book. Some may feel uncomfortable with newer words and melodies, but they are not a matter of right or wrong as long as the words are in agreement with the teaching of the Bible.

Format is based upon whether the congregation does the singing or is sung to: participators or spectators.

A change in musical formats is often attached to a plea for a change in musical idioms, or types of music. The type of music is a matter of preference. The format is a different matter. Format is the style of presentation. It is based upon whether the congregation does the singing or is sung to: participators or spectators. It is a matter of which is pleasing in God's sight: congregational singing or choral music, solos, duets, trios, and quartets.

Many people who advocate a change of musical format, or presentation, usually try to base their changes upon a faulty interpretation of the words found in Ephesians 5:19 ("speaking to yourselves") and Colossians 3:16 ("teaching and admonishing one another"). Lynn Anderson observed:

> My parents taught me it was rude to speak when someone else was speaking to me. "When we speak to another," they coached, "we take turns." Ephesians 5:19 actually says that—at least some of the time—one group of people sings while another group listens. That can happen in several different formats: solos, trios, antiphonal singing, quartets, and a rich variety of other creative formats, in addition to everybody singing at once.[23]

Along this same line of thought, some brethren argue that there is no difference in having one person read a psalm to the congregation or sing the same words as a solo. The reasoning is faulty. Preaching, or reading from the Bible, and singing are two separate acts of worship and each must have its own authority from God.

---

23. Anderson, p. 128.

Some people assert that, in most songs, everyone does not sing at the same time but that there are periods of time in a song when one group—alto, soprano, bass, or tenor—takes the lead while the other people listen. In his book *Singing and New Testament Worship,* Dave Miller addressed the problem:

> God wants the assembly to participate together in the song service. To sit quietly as a spectator is to fail to "sing one to another." When two or more individuals "sing to each other," they may not sing every word of the song simultaneously, but they will all participate in the singing of the song. Otherwise, they are not "singing to each other."[24]

First Corinthians 14:26 is an alleged proof text frequently used by those people who advocate solo singing: "each one has a psalm." Rather than urging the use of solos, Paul seemed to be rebuking those in the assembly who were not taking their turns in leading songs, speaking in tongues, or prophesying but instead were trying to speak at the same time. If this passage advocates solos, then it would be wrong to have congregational singing. Each person would have to sing a solo sometime during the assembly.

Paul seemed to be rebuking those who were not taking their turns, but instead were trying to speak at the same time.

Space is limited in this chapter, but the reader is urged to read Dave Miller's excellent book, *Singing and New Testament Worship*, to make a serious study of the reflective pronouns—*heautois* and *heautous*—that are used in a reciprocal sense in Ephesians 5:19 and Colossians 3:16.

As a schoolteacher I can understand the wisdom of the divine examples of congregational singing in the first century church. Part of our reading curriculum involved teaching the children phonics by means of rules set to music. We began each day by singing those rules. Every child had to participate in the singing, and one of my responsibilities as an instructor was to nudge those who were lazy or indifferent. It was amazing how quickly and how thoroughly the students learned the information by constant participation in the singing. God has some important principles for his children to learn by their wholehearted participation in

---

24. Dave Miller, Singing and New Testament Worship (Abilene, TX: Quality Publications, 1994), pp. 32-33.

singing praises to him. Those principles are ingrained into our subconscious minds by verbalizing them over and over in song. Listening to other people perform is not nearly as effective as active participation.

Humming and Clapping

Sometimes the question of humming a psalm, hymn, or spiritual song arises. Humming may sound pleasing to the ear, but it is not scriptural because it is not singing. God specified acceptable singing: words that offer praise as well as teach and admonish one another.

In this instance, the two hands have become percussion instruments.

The effects of the Pentecostal movement have penetrated the Lord's church in the form of clapping to the rhythm of a song while it is being sung. In this instance, the two hands have become percussion instruments. There is no difference in hitting the skin of one hand with the other and in beating time to the music with the skin of a hand and the skin of a drum. Both constitute the use of mechanical instruments of music in worship.

Conclusion

A perusal of the epistles reveals a constant problem in most of the early churches. Judaizing teachers were constantly stirring up trouble by advocating the keeping of parts of the law along with Christianity. They just could not seem to understand that Christians were no longer under the Jewish law. Today many have the same problem. Although musical instruments and choral groups were never a part of the original tabernacle worship, they were introduced by David and tolerated by Jehovah. But the supreme sacrifice of Christ removed the entire older covenant and a better one was given. The new covenant is silent concerning the use of mechanical instruments of music and only the congregational singing of psalms, hymns, and spiritual songs has been authorized.

Although Christians are no longer living under the law, characters from the Old Testament still have powerful lessons to teach us. Their messages have echoed from the walls of time since the beginning of civilization. These people, "being dead, yet [speak]."

Cain tells us that one sacrifice is not just as good as another. Nadab and Abihu warn us about substituting different kinds of fire. Uzzah reminds us that good intentions don't make an action right. The Israelites, who demanded a king so they could be like those around them, teach us that trying to conform to the world is not always the best course to take.

Cain tells us that one sacrifice is not just as good as another.

Finally, the Pharisees could teach us one of the most important lessons of all. We can carry out commands to the letter of the law and yet be completely displeasing in the sight of God. We may engage in congregational singing of scriptural songs, without the aid of mechanical instruments of music and special singing groups, and our worship will still be unacceptable if our hearts are not right. While it is necessary to spend time in warning about false teaching, we must constantly be on guard concerning our attitudes. We could win the battle and yet lose the war.

Questions

1. Contrast the differences in the old and new covenants.
2. How can we know what music was like in the church of the first century?
3. Relate the context of each of the instances in the New Testament when singing is mentioned and draw conclusions.
4. What does early church history tell us about the kind of music used by the Christians during the first few centuries?
5. After mechanical instruments of music were introduced into the worship of the church, what sort of opposition was raised by many religious people?
6. Were mechanical instruments of music in worship used by the early churches in the Restoration Movement? When were they introduced? What was the result?
7. Discuss the meaning of *psallo*.
8. What is the difference between specific and generic commands? Apply this principle to music in the worship.
9. What bearing does the mention of mechanical instruments of music in the book of Revelation have upon the way we worship today?

10. What arguments are advocated by those people who want solos, duets, trios, quartets, and choral singing groups used in the worship of the church today? Use scriptures to refute their claims.
11. Are the practices of humming and clapping during the singing of songs in worship acceptable? Defend your answer.
12. What place does attitude play in the acceptance of the music used in worship to God? What are some ways we can improve our own attitudes during worship? How can we win the battle and yet lose the war?